Meera.
It has been a tr... ...ng
with you this summer... ...l,
diligence, and thoughtfulness are great
assets. We were lucky to have you.
Good luck this year at school.
Please stay in touch.
Thanks for everything!
—Zach

IS THAT A POLITICIAN IN YOUR POCKET?

WASHINGTON ON $2 MILLION A DAY

Micah L. Sifry and Nancy Watzman

Dear Meera:
...nt you so much for all
your ...ant work!
You were such a pleasure
to work with.
I truly appreciated
... Accuracy of
your work. Thank you
for your professionalism.
...

WILEY

John Wiley & Sons, Inc.

Published by John Wiley & Sons, Inc., Hoboken, New Jersey
Published simultaneously in Canada

For general information about our other products and services, please contact our Customer Care Department within the United States at (800) 762-2974, outside the United States at (317) 572-3993 or fax (317) 572-4002.

Wiley also publishes its books in a variety of electronic formats. Some content that appears in print may not be available in electronic books. For more information about Wiley products, visit our web site at www.wiley.com.

Library of Congress Cataloging-in-Publication Data:

Sifry, Micah L.
  Is that a politician in your pocket? : Washington on $2 million a day
/ Micah L. Sifry and Nancy Watzman.
      p.   cm.
  Includes bibliographical references and index.
  ISBN 0-471-67995-X (pbk.)
  1. Lobbying—United States.   2. Pressure groups—United States.
  3. United States. Congress—Ethics.   I. Watzman, Nancy.   II. Title.
  JK1118.S573   2004
  328.73'078—dc22

                                                        2004008520

Printed in the United States of America

10 9 8 7 6 5 4 3 2 1

IF ANYONE IS GOING TO OWN THE POLITICIANS,
IT MIGHT AS WELL BE US.

Contents

ACKNOWLEDGMENTS

We have depended upon the support and help of many people to produce this book. First and foremost, Public Campaign's executive director, Nick Nyhart, gave us the time and resources to get the job done. The rest of Public Campaign's staff—Susan L. Anderson, Rick Bielke, Mark Clack, Bill Ewing, Gail Gomez, Tory Griffith, Cietta Kiandoli, Mary McClelland, Deb Ross, and Melina Sanchez—have also shown plenty of patience and provided much support. David Donnelly, political director of our sister organization Public Campaign Action Fund, has done the same. In addition, Melina helped us with research on campaign finance data at a crucial time. Our former colleagues Ellen Miller and Margaret Engle also warrant special mention: Ellen for originally encouraging us to launch our e-mail bulletins on how big money in politics affects people in their everyday lives, back in 1998, and Margaret for coming up with their evocative name: OUCH!

Other former Public Campaigners and regional partners provided inspiration and fellowship over the years, including Betty Ahrens, Karen Carpenter, Michael Ettlinger, Janet Groat, Winnett Hagens, Gail Hoffman, Jennifer Keen, Randy Kehler, Brian Leiken, Pete MacDowell, Ryan MacPherson, Bruce Miller, Addrana Montgomery, Len Norwitz, Donna Parson, Annie Perezchica, Eric Schmeltzer, Kathy Schulman, Jodie Silverman, Tracy Sturdivant, Kelly Weigle, and Dexter Wimbish. And we would be remiss not to also salute veteran reform activists Max Bartlett, Carrie Bolton, John Bonifaz, Andrew Boyd, Marc Caplan, George Christie, Doug

Clopp, Steve Cobble, Janice Fine, Becky Glass, Bob Hall, Marty Jezer, Santiago Juarez, Barb Lubin, Joan and Jay Mandle, William McNary, Stephanie Moore, John Moyers, Gwen Patton, Dan Petegorsky, Miles Rapaport, Jamin Raskin, Samantha Sanchez, Ben Senturia, Whitney North Seymour Jr., Alison Smith, and David Smith.

Beyond our own organization, we're deeply indebted to the many others in Washington and around the country devoted to watching out for the public interest on various issues: Center for American Progress, Center for Digital Democracy, Common Cause, Consumer Federation of America, Consumers Union, Earthjustice, Economic Policy Institute, Environmental Working Group, Greenpeace, National Institute on Money in State Politics, National Reinvestment Community Coalition, Natural Resources Defense Council, Public Citizen, Sierra Club, Texans for Public Justice, and U.S. PIRG. This is just a partial list of groups whose research proved invaluable for the writing of this book. In addition, we owe a great deal to investigative journalists and organizations who have dug deeply into many of the issues covered within, including Donald Barlett and James Steele of *Time,* Carl Prine of the *Pittsburgh Tribune-Review,* David Willman of the *Los Angeles Times,* Charles Lewis and the Center for Public Integrity, and PBS's *Frontline.* Our friends and colleagues Marc Cooper, David Corn, Paul Cuadros, Arianna Huffington, Doug Ireland, and Katrina vanden Heuvel were also very supportive.

A special mention must go to Sheila Krumholz and Doug Weber of the Center for Responsive Politics, without whom we couldn't have written this book. At a time when the money cascading into politics seems to have grown into an incomprehensible flood, the center performs a vital service in helping the public understand who is trying to buy whom. Long may it run!

Likewise, we must thank Bill Moyers and the Schumann Center for Media and Democracy, both for pushing us initially to consider turning all those OUCH! bulletins into a book, and then for providing critical early support so we could flesh out the whole picture. They have been long-distance runners in a field not for the short-winded, along with Public Campaign's good friends Jackie

Berrien at the Ford Foundation; Michael Caudell-Feagan at the Proteus Fund; Susan Clark of the Columbia Foundation; the Compton Family; Arnold Hiatt of the Stride-Rite Foundation; Steven Kirsch, Kathi Gwynn, and Susan Frank at the Steven and Michelle Kirsch Foundation; Geri Mannion at the Carnegie Foundation; and Mark Schmitt at the Open Society Institute.

Thanks to Kim Witherspoon and David Forrer of Witherspoon Associates for seeing the value in this project and helping bring it to fruition. Eric Nelson of John Wiley & Sons, our editor, has been an author's dream: committed from the beginning, enthusiastic, patient, inspired, and inspiring. And thanks to Alexa Selph and Marcia Samuels, our copy editor and production editor, for doing such a bang-up job on getting the book in print so quickly.

If we could say with a pictogram how much it has meant to us to collaborate with our graphic designer, Chris Foss, the image would be an anchor. Chris has been with us from day one as we developed this book, and his contributions go far beyond the visual depictions of quantitative information that illuminate our text.

Finally, we'd like to thank our families, who so lovingly allowed us to devote many of our evenings and weekends in recent months to this book—Nancy's husband, Mark Nitczynski, and her parents, June and Whitey Watzman, and Micah's wife, Leslie, and their kids, Mira and Jesse, along with the rest of our extended *mishpoches*.

A note to readers: For reasons of space, we have left endnotes out of the print version. To read and download a complete set of endnotes, go to our Web site at **www.publicampaign.org.**

OUCH! HOW MONEY IN POLITICS HURTS YOU

The alarm clock rings. You hit the snooze button. Get out of bed. Pull on some clothes. Make coffee. Transfer some chicken from the freezer to the refrigerator so it will defrost during the day. Feed the baby some mashed peaches. You make a mental note to yourself: tonight you have to pay bills. You got a notice from the cable company yesterday, you're overdue. Afterwards, you round up the kids and climb into the SUV to take them to school. You have to remind your fifth grader to bring her asthma inhaler, as she's always "forgetting" it at home because she's embarrassed about it.

What does your morning have to do with politics? With elections? With democracy? With the CEO of the media conglomerate who lives several miles away in a palatial home, who dined last night on truffled foie gras and champagne with the local candidate for the U.S. Senate, while you and the kids were chowing on macaroni and cheese?

Plenty.

You may not think about it much as you go through your day, but our campaign finance system, in which special interest cash governs who runs for office, how they conduct their campaigns, and what they do (and don't do) once elected, touches on nearly every aspect of our lives. The air we breathe, the food we eat, the health care we receive (or don't receive), all of these are affected, and for the worse, by the influence of money in politics.

That teaspoon of sugar you stirred into your coffee? It's overpriced, thanks to a decades-old federal sugar subsidy program. For years, sugar interests have beaten back attempts to reform the system, and they've gotten their way, thanks to more than $20 million in campaign contributions since 1989.

The chicken you are defrosting? It may be infected with deadly bacteria, such as salmonella or listeria. If it is, there's a good chance that the feds know that the plant that processed it has had a list of sanitary violations a mile long—but it doesn't matter, because they lack the authority to shut it down. The livestock, poultry, and food processing industries, who have contributed more than $101 million since 1989, have successfully fought all attempts to give the government this power.

Those mashed peaches that you fed the baby? They contained chlorothalonil, a fungicide classified by the Environmental Protection Agency (EPA) as a likely carcinogen, as well as a dose of methomyl, a neurotoxin. Consumer groups charge that the agency is not setting standards for pesticide exposure that are protective enough for kids, whose small bodies are more vulnerable to harmful effects from the chemicals than adults are. Agriculture chemical manufacturers have contributed $7.1 million since 1989.

The cable bill? It has climbed at three times the rate of inflation since Congress passed the Telecommunications Act of 1996, which was supposed to open up competition within the communications sector and bring prices down for consumers. Instead, the deregulatory law encouraged a handful of large companies to continue to monopolize the market. Cable companies have contributed more than $32 million since 1989.

The SUV? There is a glut on the market of these huge cars, which get notoriously poor mileage. More gas burned means that more carbon dioxide, a major contributor to the greenhouse effect, gets pumped into into the atmosphere. The technology exists to improve the fuel efficiency of SUVs. However, for years, the automotive industry, the source of more than $90 million in campaign contributions since 1989, has successfully blocked efforts to raise fuel efficiency standards for SUVs and other light trucks.

And the asthma inhaler? Studies show that as air pollution increases, children's asthma rates increase. President George W. Bush, who has collected more than $1.1 million from electric utilities for his two presidential campaigns, has issued regulations that weaken the Clean Air Act, by permitting utilities to update their plants without installing new, more efficient, emissions controls. Over all, electric utilities have contributed more than $86 million to federal campaigns since 1989.

OUCH!

In 1998 Public Campaign launched "OUCH! How Money in Politics Hurts You," an e-mail bulletin covering the everyday outrages that result when the only way to run for office is either to be rich, or to know lots of rich people to finance your campaign. After six years of publication, we have a pile of OUCHes tall enough that we feel pretty bruised and battered. In this book we gather them together and elaborate upon them to show how the campaign finance system affects all of us in our everyday lives.

We will show you how a couple hundred million dollars in campaign contributions from the securities, accounting, banking, and high-tech industries defanged the government regulators and ripped out the stops on corporate greed, enriching a handful of insiders at the top and trashing the retirement plans of millions of small investors. We will show you how Americans pay more for cable TV, prescription drugs, and basic commodities; how the safety of our food, children's health, and travel is compromised; how we shell out more in taxes to prop up timber and mining industries and banking moguls—even how we're less safe than we could be from terrorist attacks.

All of this happens because wealthy special interests buy favors from Congress and the White House with their campaign contributions. Do you have a politician in your pocket? Unlikely, unless you have lots of cash in there too. Campaign money is the fuel that politicians need to run their campaigns, and if you are not contributing, then they are less likely to pay attention to your concerns, especially when your interests are competing with wealthy special interests.

Every day, they pump another $2 million into the bank accounts of our elected representatives and their political party committees—hence the subtitle of our book, *Washington on $2 Million a*

Day. This money isn't coming from people like you and me—95 percent of all Americans can't afford, or don't bother, to make campaign contributions. The bulk of the real money, donations of $200 or more, comes from an even tinier fraction of the country, just one-quarter of one percent of the population. No wonder so many of the benefits of government—tax breaks, regulatory relief, subsidies and boondoggles—flow into their laps. Meanwhile, the rest of us pay in all kinds of real ways.

But don't despair. In this book, we will also show you how we can treat ourselves for these OUCHes with the Clean Money/Clean Elections approach to elections. Under Clean Money/Clean Elections, candidates who meet certain strict requirements to prove their support qualify to receive public funds if they promise to refuse private contributions and abide by spending limits. Versions of Clean Money/Clean Elections have already passed in Arizona, Maine, Massachusetts, North Carolina, New Mexico, and Vermont, with more states on the way. Clean Money is hardly a cure-all, but it could do a great deal to help heal our body politic.

WHO'S BUYING WHOM: HOW MONEY IN POLITICS REALLY WORKS

Money has always played a prominent role in American politics. Reasonable people may disagree over whether its influence is greater or less than in the past, but today, thanks to laws requiring extensive disclosure of campaign contributions, we can clearly document how money, not votes, is the primary currency of democracy.

Money Buys You Viability

Why does money play such an important role in who gets elected and in what policies they will champion? The answer is simple: candidates need money to run effective campaigns—to hire staff, print materials, run ads on TV and radio, and coordinate volunteers. It cost $5 million, on average, to win a Senate seat in 2002. It cost just over $966,000 to win a House seat. Six years earlier, the average Senate winner spent $4.7 million, the average House winner $674,000. If you were a challenger running against an incumbent in 2002, you needed even more money to win—almost $1.6 million for House candidates. In the House the average challenger had less than one-quarter the funding of the average incumbent in 2002. In the Senate the average challenger had barely one-sixth

THE PRICE OF WINNING
1996 vs 2002

$5,000,000
$4,700,000

$966,000
$674,000

HOUSE SEAT   **SENATE SEAT**

Source: CRP

5

the war chest. That's one big reason so few incumbents ever lose their seats, along with the partisan gerrymandering that guarantees most of them a safe ride to reelection if they aren't challenged in a primary. (The same dynamic occurs at the state level, by the way, where a winning candidate for state senate or assembly can spend over $1 million.)

So say you want to run for Congress. If you aren't wealthy yourself, like Senator Jon Corzine (D-NJ), an investment banker who spent over $60 million of his own money on his 2000 election campaign, you have to collect the cash from other sources. Any idea where you might find a million dollars to finance a competitive bid for the House? Think about how hard it is for your local neighborhood group to raise money for its activities. Then imagine trying to do this for yourself. After you've tapped your family and friends, whom else will you turn to? Since there is no public financing available for federal candidates, the only sources for the kind of cash you will need are wealthy economic interests: the oil companies, the banks, the insurance companies, the securities firms, the utilities, the airline industry, the pharmaceutical companies, real estate interests, and so on.

Economic Interests Give the Most

Of the more than $11 billion contributed to federal candidates and parties since 1989, it's instructive to look at where most of it comes from and where it goes. The chart on the next page is based on data developed by the Center for Responsive Politics, a nonprofit, nonpartisan organization that has been tracking campaign finance contributions for the last twenty years. The center downloads the raw data reported by candidates, Political Action Committees (PACs), and party committees to the Federal Election Commission (FEC), and then codes those contributions by industry and interest. By law, every contribution of more than $200 is supposed to include the donor's name, address, occupation, and employer. The center supplements that data with its own careful tracking of spouses and family members, since big donors often add to their giving by seeing to it that their relatives also make contributions. (That's totally legal, by the way.) The center also does its best to classify corporate conglomerates that may have interests in several sectors of the economy, and to separately code contributions from clearly identified subsidiaries wherever possible.

As a rule throughout this book, wherever you see statistics for a particular company, industry, or individual's campaign contributions, our source is the Center for Responsive Politics, unless otherwise noted. One important note: when we state that a particular company or industry gave a certain dollar amount to candidates and party committees, we are using shorthand to refer to the company's or industry's executives, their family members, and related Political Action Committee(s). The only exception to this rule is in soft money totals. Until soft money contributions to federal parties were recently banned, companies often gave such donations

CONTRIBUTIONS BY INDUSTRY, 1989–2004

Source: CRP; indivs ($200+), PACs, soft-money contributions to federal candidates and parties

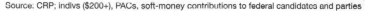

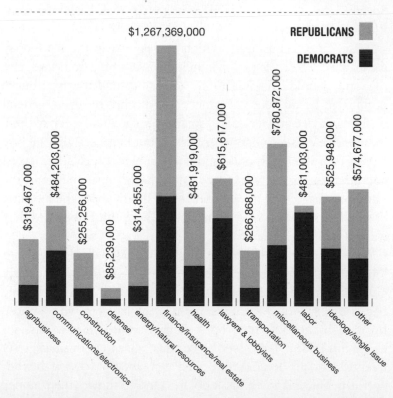

directly to party committees. The figures quoted in this book for the 2004 election cycle were downloaded by CRP from the FEC in January–March 2004. You can do your own money-in-politics research by going to the center's award-winning Web site **www.opensecrets.org**.

As you can see from this chart, one sector of the economy—the finance, insurance, and real estate sector—towers over all the others, contributing well over $1 billion since 1989. Think "Wall Street" as shorthand for this sector, though not just the part that is based in lower Manhattan. We're talking about many of the richest and most powerful businesses in the country—commercial banks, insurance companies, securities traders, accountants, real estate developers and brokers, and a group of wealthy people who modestly list their occupation as "investor." Taxes are an all-consuming interest for these people, as are government regulation of their deal making and, for some, the prospect of privatizing Social Security (and driving more lucrative stock-brokering commissions their way).

"Miscellaneous business," which comes next in the big money game, is a catchall category that includes everything from steel, textile, and chemical manufacturers to casinos and tourism, but is dominated by the food, beverage, and alcohol business; general business service providers; and small manufacturers. Each of these industries has its own narrow concerns, but in general they all care a great deal about corporate and environmental regulation, taxes, and labor issues like workplace safety, health insurance, and the minimum wage. And in case there's any doubt about the meaning of that last sentence—they care about those things because they want less of all of them.

Next in our political bestiary is another catchall: "lawyers and lobbyists." Lawyers constitute one of the few sectors that regularly give more money to Democrats than Republicans. That's largely because this group includes many trial lawyers who oppose business-backed efforts to limit damage awards in lawsuits, so-called tort reform. Lobbyists, by contrast, give to both sides pretty freely, essentially because they need to maintain access with whoever is in office. If anything, lobbyists tend to shower their money on incumbents, since they're the ones with power. Furthermore, the $79.3 million attributed to lobbyists is undoubtedly an undercount, since the federal definition is too narrow and leaves out people who conduct public relations campaigns to pressure Congress, as well as so-called strategic advisors, often former members of Congress or other ex-government officials, who give guidance on lobbying campaigns but personally don't register as lobbyists.

The next sector isn't an industry at all—it's organized labor. Historically, unions have been closely allied with the Democratic Party, and their contribution patterns prove that. Ninety-three percent of the nearly half a billion dollars that labor has contributed to parties and candidates since 1989 has gone to Democrats. That may sound like a lot of clout, but as you'll see from later chapters on the minimum wage and worker safety, labor is outspent by business by over 14 to 1 and rarely gets its way.

After labor, but still in the half-billion-dollar heavyweight category, is communications and electronics. This is the fastest growing of all the different industry sectors in terms of political contributions, in part due to the rise of the computer industry, which has quadrupled its giving since 1998. The different components of this sector show different patterns in their contributions. Hollywood—TV, movie and music producers—tilts 2 to 1 Democratic. Silicon Valley, which includes companies like Seattle-based Microsoft and Texas-based Dell, splits its money evenly. So do telecom, cable, and satellite TV—all of whom want less government regulation of their businesses (and more regulation of their competitors). Some TV and radio broadcasters, like Rupert Murdoch's News Corporation and Clear Channel, tilt 2 to 1 Republican in their giving.

The last of the half-billion-dollar donors is health care, a giant part of the economy and one that benefits in all sorts of ways from government programs and policies. Doctors, hospitals, and nursing homes are all huge recipients of Medicare and Medicaid money, and they are all highly sensitive to any proposed changes in those arrangements. The pharmaceutical companies are eager investors in politicians, since they have so much at stake in keeping drug prices unregulated. Interestingly, as HMOs and other insurance companies have gained power over doctors and other health care

A Money-in-Politics Glossary

Contribution limit: Under federal law, contributions to candidates, party committees, and Political Action Committees (PACs) are subject to limits. Before passage of the Bipartisan Campaign Reform Act, individuals were permitted to contribute a total of $2,000 to a candidate ($1,000 for the primary, $1,000 for the general election). The law hiked the limits, and now an individual may give up to $4,000 per election to a federal candidate for office; $25,000 per year to a federal party committee, such as the Republican National Committee or the Democratic National Committee; and $5,000 to a Political Action Committee (PAC). PACs may contribute $5,000 per election to federal candidates and $15,000 per year to national party committees.

Hard money: These are campaign contributions that fall under the federal contribution limit rules. Federal candidates and party committees are restricted to raising and spending hard money for campaigns. Hard money must be used for what's known as "express advocacy," for example, advertisements that urge the general public to vote for or against a candidate. All of this money must be disclosed to the Federal Election Commission, but only contributions over $200 are itemized with the name and address of donors.

Bundling: Because of the limits on hard money, political fund-raisers have become adept at the art of "bundling." It is not uncommon to see a dozen executives from a particular company each contributing to the same candidate on the same day, a classic example of bundling. Bush's Pioneers and Rangers are bundlers extraordinaire, promising to go out and raise $100,000 or $200,000 in chunks of $2,000 from others. In the 2004 elections there were rumors of an even more exalted group of Bush bundlers, who promise to raise $500,000. John Kerry has a similar, though smaller, group of campaign "vice chairs," who raise at least $100,000, and "co-chairs," who raise at least $50,000, for his war chest.

Soft money: The Bipartisan Campaign Reform Act, which went into effect for the 2004 elections, eliminated "party" soft money, the loophole in campaign finance laws that allowed wealthy individuals and corporations to lavish unlimited contributions upon the national political parties. The parties became adept at using this money to run multimillion-dollar "issue" advertising campaigns that avoided saying "vote for" or "vote against" but for all practical purposes served as campaign ads for candidates. In this election, much of this money is now flowing to independent "527" committees (so named for their place in the IRS tax code), which are allowed to spend it on influencing elections as long as they don't coordinate with any candidate or political party.

Political Action Committee: Political Action Committees (PACs) are organizations devoted to raising and spending money subject to hard money contribution limits to elect or defeat candidates. Most PACs are organized by corporations or trade associations, labor unions, or ideological groups. PACs often have feel-good names that make it tough to figure out who is really behind them, such as Americans for Responsible Leadership, which is a leadership PAC for Senator Evan Bayh (D-IN).

Leadership PAC: Politicians often form leadership PACs, which they use to contribute to other congressional candidates' campaigns, often as a way to curry favor if they aspire to a leadership position within Congress or plan to run for president. For special interests, leadership PACs offer yet another way to contribute more money to a candidate while remaining within legal limits.

providers, the latter group has started shifting its giving toward the Democrats. But overall, this sector, like every other industry, still gives more of its money to Republicans.

The other big money-givers—agribusiness, energy and natural resource companies, transportation, construction, and defense—all tilt heavily toward the Republicans. That's because Republicans are in power and the owners and executives from these industries tend to agree with Republicans on issues like taxes and regulatory policy. But until the mid-1990s, when Democrats lost control of the House of Representatives, most industries weren't quite so partisan in their giving. Congressional Democrats had gotten quite good at wooing—some might say extorting—contributions from business, since they had a great deal of power over legislation. But since the GOP rise in the House, and especially since its sweep of both chambers in recent years, big money from business has gone where the power is.

Speaking of going where the power is, in several places in this book, you'll find charts showing how a particular industry has been funneling campaign cash to major party candidates in the 2004 presidential race. These charts show three things: first, that wealthy special interests are continuing to try to curry favor with whoever will occupy the White House; second, that the general rule holds that the incumbent collects the lion's share of the campaign cash because moneyed interests are attracted to power and need to buy access; and third, that all the candidates are sadly dependent on money from wealthy interests in order to run competitive campaigns. These charts demonstrate yet again why comprehensive campaign reform is sorely needed.

One surprise about this overall picture: where are those "special interest" groups that we hear so much about? A lot of people tend to think of special interests as any organized, politically active group they personally disagree with, whether it's the Sierra Club or the ACLU on the one hand or the National Right to Life Committee and the Eagle Forum on the other. But while a few of these ideological groups are modest-sized players in the campaign contributing game, it is important to remember that they are utterly, totally, undeniably dwarfed by the economic interests described above. Reasonable people may have different opinions about ideologically charged issues such as gay marriage or abortion or foreign policy. But the banks, insurance companies, hospitals, HMOs, chemical manufacturers, and so forth are the real special interests, because they are working from a strict profit motive. They are buying politicians because it helps their bottom line, not because they genuinely believe that tax shelters are good for the public interest.

Do they always triumph? Of course not. Once in a blue moon, especially if the media focus on a particular travesty, they lose. The defeat of Big Tobacco, which tried to get Congress to give it tens of billions of dollars to defray the cost of its quarter-trillion-dollar settlement with the states, is one such example. But most of the time, public interest groups are vastly outgunned on Capitol Hill. So when you hear the words *special interest*—perhaps it would be wisest to look primarily at those narrow interests who lobby Washington every day, and who paper it with the most money.

Demographics of the Donor Class

So far, we've looked at big money in politics by categorizing the givers of money by the industry they come from. But just who are the people who actually write the checks, the ones who get to "vote" before anybody else gets a chance, and who, to paraphrase George Orwell in his classic *Animal Farm*, are "more equal than

The Donor Class

Odds are excellent that you, dear reader, are not a big campaign contributor. Just about one-quarter of one percent of the total U.S. population, that is, just 651,739 out of a population of some 288 million, made a contribution of over $200 to a federal candidate or party in the 2002 elections, according to the Center for Responsive Politics. Turn that around and you see that means that 99.8 percent of the population did not make a political contribution of this amount.

If you did:

- You're probably richer than most. One out of five political donors makes $500,000 a year, and another three out of five make over $100,000, according to a 1998 survey of big givers done by a group of academic experts supported by the Joyce Foundation. Fewer than one out of ten Americans make over $100,000.

- You are probably white. Ninety-five percent of political donors are white, according to the same survey.

- You are also probably male. Eighty percent of political donors are male.

- Chances are, you live in Washington, D.C., New York City, or Los Angeles. The zip code 20005, in Washington, D.C., is home base to many well-heeled lobbyists and, as such, provided more campaign cash during the 2002 elections than did contributors from thirty-three different states. Other zip codes that are big sources of campaign money include 10021, in Manhattan's Upper East Side, and 90210, in Beverly Hills, California.

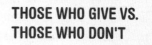

THOSE WHO GIVE VS. THOSE WHO DON'T

If an entire page of this book represents the total U.S. population, this dot represents the 0.2% that gives $200 or more.

Source: CRP

others"? Here's what we know about the demographics of political givers: they're more likely to be white, wealthy, older, and more conservative than the average American.

Small Donors Scarcely Count

Some trends in political money giving are also important to note. Perhaps the most important one is this: small donors matter less and less. In 1996 "hard money" (see glossary) donations of $200 or less—the kind that don't require the disclosure of individual donor information by the FEC—amounted to $734 million. That was one-third of all the money raised for that election cycle, which amounted to $2.4 billion. Four years later, in 2000, small hard money contributions amounted to only $550 million. Not only was this an absolute drop of 25 percent in the amount coming from "the little people," it also was a smaller proportion of the total amount raised in the 2000 election cycle; that is, contributions from small donors amounted to barely 19 percent of the $2.9 billion raised that year.

It's possible that the close presidential contest of 2004 and the growing role of the Internet in political fund-raising will moderate that trend somewhat. When Democratic candidate Howard Dean was riding high, raising a record amount of over $47 million, the experts were astounded by the fact that 60 percent of his money came from donors giving $200 or less. He talked often of finding two million people who would give $100 each, an unheard-of achievement if he could have pulled it off. But while small contributors may be coming back in larger numbers this time around, the early data suggest that the overall trend won't change much and most of the money raised will actually come from big check-writers.

Indeed, while President Bush was

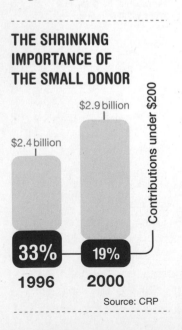

THE SHRINKING IMPORTANCE OF THE SMALL DONOR

Contributions under $200

$2.9 billion

$2.4 billion

33% 19%

1996 2000

Source: CRP

vastly outraising Senator John Kerry—$158.8 million to $41.4 million reported as of March 20, 2004, a $100 million–plus advantage that even Kerry supporters admitted couldn't be closed—there was one similarity between the two men's fund-raising. Both were heavily dependent on people who were giving the maximum allowable individual contribution to their campaigns. In Bush's case, two-thirds of his money had come from donors giving $2,000 each. In Kerry's case, just under half of his money had come from those givers.

The Color of Money

A second critical fact about the donor class is how unrepresentative it is of America's diverse population. An examination of individual contributions to federal candidates, parties, and Political Action Committees (PACs) in the last two elections shows that 9 out of 10 dollars of those contributions exceeding $200 came from majority non-Hispanic white zip codes.

Yet nearly one out of three Americans is a person of color. Just 1.8 percent of those campaign funds came from predominantly Latino zip codes, 2.8 percent from predominantly African American zip codes, and 0.6 percent from predominantly Asian Pacific American neighborhoods. These facts come from "The Color of Money," a groundbreaking study that Public Campaign conducted with two civil rights groups, the Fannie Lou Hamer Project and the William Velasquez Institute. By comparing U.S. Census data on the racial, ethnic, and class makeup of more than 25,000 zip codes in the country to the more than $2 billion in itemized campaign contributions made in 2000 and 2002, we also found that:

THE COLOR OF MONEY
2000 & 2002 ELECTIONS

89.5%

% CONTRIBUTIONS FROM
MAJORITY NON-HISPANIC
WHITE ZIP CODES

Source: ColorofMoney.org

• The top contributing zip code nationwide—10021, on Manhattan's exclusive Upper East Side—was the source of $28.4 million for federal campaigns in the 2002 and 2000 elections, and is home to 91,514 people ages 18 and over, 86 percent of whom are non-Hispanic white. Nearly 40 percent of the households have incomes of $100,000 or more.

- The neighborhoods supplying most of the money for federal campaigns in this country are also among the nation's wealthiest. Nearly one out of two federal individual campaign dollars ($200+)—$991 million—came from a person living in a wealthy zip code (defined as one where the percentage of households making over $100,000 per year is twice the national average).
- Just 12 percent of the adult population lives in these neighborhoods. Meanwhile, just 5.9 percent of individual campaign dollars—$118.8 million—comes from poor neighborhoods (defined as those where the percentage of households below the poverty level is twice the national average). Nearly 9 percent of adult Americans live in these communities.

Another way to look at it: individuals living in wealthy neighborhoods supply eight dollars for every one dollar that people living in poor communities give to federal campaigns.

These disparities play out starkly across America's states and cities. In California, where nearly one out of two residents is a person of color, 85 percent of the campaign cash comes from zip codes that are predominantly non-Hispanic white. In New York City, more than half the population is people of color, but 93 percent of the campaign cash comes from non-Hispanic white zip codes. (To find out how your zip code shapes up, go to our interactive Web site at **www.colorofmoney.org**.)

Everyone Is on a Money Chase

When a candidate is forced to spend so much time hunting for money in the nation's wealthiest neighborhoods, it also affects his view of the nation and public policy. "Inevitably, as the politician enters into the endless round of coffees, meals, and receptions among the networks of the wealthy, his view of the world is reframed," wrote former labor secretary Robert Reich in a 1997 piece for the *New Yorker*.

> Increasingly, the politician hears the same kind of suggestions, the same voicing of concerns and priorities. The wealthy do not speak in one voice, to be sure, but they share a broad common perspective in which such things as balancing the budget, opening trade routes, and cutting taxes on capital gains are of central importance. Meanwhile, the politician hears only indirectly and abstractly from the less comfortable members of society. The pollster shows him how focus groups of average, working-class people have answered a blizzard of questions. But the less comfortable are not at the coffees and dinners with the politician. They do not play golf with him. They do not tell the politician directly and repeatedly in casual banter or through personal stories, how they view the world. They do not speak continuously into the politician's ear about such concerns as job security, wages, child care, the cost of housing and health insurance, and mounting credit card debt.

"Access to the network of the wealthy does not buy a politician's mind; instead, it nibbles constantly, sweetly, at his ear," Reich concluded.

Former U.S. senator and presidential candidate Bill Bradley (D-NJ) agrees. Constant fund-raising, he told journalist Matt Miller, "drains people's time and energy from being able to focus on these issues and fills it up with catering to the rich." And all that time spent among rich people subtly alters their worldview. "By raising money, they associate with a whole new class of people and they like it. They personalize their political bank account, and it comes in their subconscious to be their own personal bank account. They've raised $10 million. Here's this guy they're with on a family yacht. There's a certain comparability there." Bradley concludes: "That is the most corrupting aspect of this process."

Most candidates also have to spend a ridiculous amount of time raising money. About one-quarter of candidates running for the U.S. House or statewide offices say they spend more than half their time raising money. A similar percentage said they spend between one-quarter and one-half of their time on fund-raising. That's time not spent talking to average voters over their kitchen tables. And it can't help but have an invidious effect.

The Wealth Primary

Because money is so important in most high-level elections, there is a kind of "wealth primary" that occurs before anyone gets to cast a vote. Candidates who raise a lot of cash early are considered "viable." Those who don't, aren't, and often the media simply write those candidates out of the picture. As a result, the narrow class of people who give substantial sums of money to candidates for office gets to subtly shape the field of people running. Not only that, their interests are bound to count more than the interests of average voters.

Consider the presidency. In 1999 then-candidate George W. Bush shocked the political establishment by raising an unheard of $37 million by the end of June, a full six months before anyone in Iowa, New Hampshire, or anywhere else would be voting. He opted not to participate in the partial public financing system for presidential races, which would have required him to abide by spending limits, and went on to raise $101 million for his primary race, more than twice the amount raised by his most serious rival, John McCain. The other Republicans, such as Dan Quayle, John Kasich, and Elizabeth Dole, who also had dreams of calling the White House home, didn't stand a chance.

They knew it, too. Here's what John Kasich, whose experience included nearly a decade in Congress, several of those as chairman of the powerful House Budget Committee, had to say the day he realized his campaign wasn't going anywhere: "When you raise $600,000 in one quarter and someone else raises $30 million, it's a wake-up call. With such limited resources, we couldn't have competed."

When former labor secretary Elizabeth Dole dropped out of the race for the presidential nomination, she said: "I've learned that the current political calendar and election laws favor those who get an early start and can tap into huge private fortunes, or who have a pre-existing network of political supporters." She added that her campaign made her realize that ideas meant nothing without money. (She learned her lesson: in her successful run for North Carolina's open Senate seat in 2002, she spent $13.7 million, a hair more than her opponent, Erskine Bowles, who spent $13.2 million.)

Tennessee governor Lamar Alexander, whose bid for the presidency also failed to catch on, said after quitting, "If there were something we need to change in the process . . . it would be to make it less reliant on money."

The experience of 2000 made a profound impression, and candidates in 2004 have followed the Bush blueprint. To be "viable," presidential hopefuls such as John Kerry, Joe Lieberman, John Edwards, Richard Gephardt, and Howard Dean spent most of 2003 trying to raise the $25 million political pros all said was necessary to survive the early presidential primaries. The candidates who failed to clear that money hurdle never got serious attention from the press. And in the end, faced with President Bush's precedent-busting decision to opt out of the partial public financing system for presidential campaigns and thus not have any limits on how much he could spend on the primaries, both Democratic front-runners, Dean and Kerry, opted out too.

The Bottom Line

At the end of the day, there are only two questions that you need to ask about money in politics. First, what does it cost us? The rest of this book will give you answers to that in detail. But consider this. No one disputes that Washington wastes huge sums of taxpayer money on corporate welfare. Estimates vary: The libertarian Cato Institute says about $65 billion a year; the liberal group Public Citizen says $150 billion a year. A few years ago, *Money* magazine estimated that each household pays nearly $1,600 per year for legislation benefiting corporations and the wealthy—some $160 billion in special tax breaks, subsidies, and other cushy deals—purchased by our system of privately financed campaigns.

The second question is, whose money is going to be in politics? No one claims, anymore at least, that there's any way to get money out of politics. It will always search for paths to influence. Nor should we imagine that getting all the money out of politics is a necessary goal. The real issues are, where is the money coming from and what kinds of strings are attached to it? In our opinion, the best solution to all the problems raised by private money in politics isn't to try to write tighter and more complicated regulations on its use; it is to create an alternative source of clean, disinterested public money for candidates who want to be able to run a viable campaign for office without being dependent on any private donors. That idea isn't a pipe dream, by the way. Known as "Clean Money/Clean Elections," or "Voter-Owned Elections" or "Impartial Justice" (when it's applied to the financing of judicial elections), it's already the law in five states, with more on the way. In our concluding chapter, we'll explain how it works and why it is the wave of the future.

Five Myths about Money in Politics

Myth No. 1. The public doesn't care about campaign finance reform. We're told—usually by those with a vested political or ideological interest in preventing reform—that campaign finance is of no concern to most people, and therefore lawmakers don't need to act. It's true that as an abstract issue, campaign finance reform ranks lower than the economy or health care or improving education as a priority for most Americans. But when people make the connection between issues like tax fairness or the quality of health care, they understand the need for reform. Numerous polls have found overwhelming majorities who want a fundamental overhaul of the way political campaigns are financed.

Myth No. 2. All we need is full and immediate electronic disclosure. Disclosure is the bedrock of our current system. That's how we know who's trying to buy whom. And though it could be improved by mandating electronic filing (a no-brainer in the current age of computer technology), without additional analysis, voters would be buried in a blizzard of data. As Mark Schmitt, policy director for former U.S. senator Bill Bradley, has noted, "Instant disclosure is useless to voters without a lot of additional information to put it in context. A lot of related information, such as what legislative action a contributor is interested in, doesn't become available until well after the election."

This type of "reform" would only further muddle the picture that voters already see: there's too much special interest money in the system and lawmakers are puppets in big contributors' hands.

Myth No. 3. More, not less, money should be spent on campaigns. If we count clichés alone, this should be better known as the Potato Chip Argument, as in, "More money is spent by Americans buying potato chips than is spent on elections." Enemies of reform love to make this argument, which was first popularized by an academic named Bradley Smith in a libertarian magazine. Smith is now the Republican-appointed chair of the Federal Election Commission. This is a classic apples-and-oranges trick. Such comparisons ignore the fact that the market for potato chips is a lot bigger than the market for votes. America's 100 million or so adult voters are offered a choice of their representatives only once every two years, whereas a far larger pool of consumers buys millions of bags of potato chips every day. Besides, if more money was spent on campaigns, would voters be better informed? Not likely. With negative advertising, more money would likely lead to increased voter alienation. Most important, since the vast majority of money that finances campaigns comes from special interests, this "deform" would increase their hold on lawmakers.

Myth No. 4. The problem was solved by eliminating party soft money. It's true, the unlimited donations from corporations, unions, and rich individuals to the parties had become an endless funnel of special interest money that undermined all the limits in the law. Shutting national party soft money down, which was achieved by the Bipartisan Campaign Reform Act of 2002, was a critical first step. But eliminating it did not address the day-to-day special interest financing that has

* * * * *

"The incessant money chase that permeates every crevice of our political system is like an unending circular marathon. And it is a race that sends a clear message to the people: that it is money, money, money that reigns supreme in American politics."

—*Senator Robert Byrd (D-WV),* March 1997 floor speech

corrupted Congress and its lawmaking. Even with soft money's extraordinary explosion in 2000, it still accounted for only 16 percent of the total amount of money spent. The other 84 percent also came overwhelmingly from wealthy individuals and corporate interests—as did most of the money fueling political campaigns before the soft money loophole was invented. And while one $2,000 hard money donation may comprise a small percentage of a candidate's total war chest, the combined effect of one such contribution bundled with many others from donors representing the same industry or interest group is significant indeed.

Myth No. 5. Ideology matters more than money in affecting votes on policy. Many members of Congress don't need to be persuaded by a timely contribution from a special interest in order to vote with that interest's position. Politicians who are probusiness and anti-regulation are going to attract contributions from industries and individuals who favor those policies. The money can't be said, in the strict sense, to have bought their vote. But this misses the point in two ways. First of all, the need to raise money to run a viable campaign, and its availability from a narrow, skewed portion of the electorate, means that the pool of successful candidates will invariably tilt toward the interests of big money. Second, on many votes a member of Congress may not be hearing much from the public at all (because the media pay little attention most of the time), but he or she is hearing a lot from the special interests who are seeking some favor or subsidy. It's when we the people are paying the least attention that big money matters the most. Even FEC chair Bradley Smith, who opposes most campaign finance regulation, has admitted that "campaign contributions have [a] meaningful effect on legislative voting behavior . . . on a limited number of votes that are generally related to technical issues arousing little public interest." Of course, one person's "technical issue" can be someone else's boondoggle or tax break.

PART ONE

OUR POCKETS ARE BEING PICKED

"We must keep the lines of communication open if we want to continue passing legislation that will benefit your industry."

—April 9, 1999, letter from **Jim Nicholson, then chair of the Republican National Committee,** to Charles Heimbold Jr., then chief executive of Bristol-Myers. The company and its employees have given over $4 million to federal candidates and party committees since 1999, over 80% to Republicans. Heimbold is now the U.S. ambassador to Sweden.

RX: RIP-OFF—HOW BIG PHARMA STAYS ON TOP

More than 1 in 5 Americans lack insurance for prescription drugs, and more than 1 in 3 seniors often skip taking their medication due to high costs. Yet Congress seems more addicted to pharmaceutical industry cash than it is devoted to helping ordinary people get affordable drugs. The new Medicare prescription drug benefit is a case in point.

If it weren't for the free drug samples that the doctors at an outpatient health clinic give away, 73-year-old Mary Fallacaro of Howard Beach, New York, would have no way to obtain the prescription drugs that she needs to deal with Alzheimer's disease and high cholesterol. "My mother only has a certain amount of income from Social Security, which covers her mortgage," her daughter, Anna Marie Martire, recently told *Newsday*. "Without these pills, she couldn't survive."

Fallacaro is just one example of the millions of Americans who aren't able to afford the medications they need. A 69-year-old man named Leonard, who didn't want to give his last name to the newspaper, relies on free samples from his doctors, too. "It's depressing to ask," he says. "You feel like a beggar—have you got any medication this month? You don't feel right. But it's just so expensive that you can't afford it."

More than one in five Americans lack insurance for prescription drugs, including over 7 million senior citizens. Most of these seniors make less than $21,000 a year. In addition, over a third of seniors with drug benefits report not filling prescriptions or skipping doses due to their high costs. At the same time, seniors are more reliant on vital medicines than ever, and drug prices have been climbing by at least 10 percent a year since the early 1990s. The average Medicare beneficiary spent a little over $2,300 out-of-pocket on prescription drugs in 2003. One out of six spent over $4,000!

If only senior citizens could spend the same amount of money on buying access and influence in Washington!

Since 1989 pharmaceutical manufacturers and related health products companies have been the source of $108.4 million to federal candidates and parties. Two-thirds of that total was given to Republicans, according to the Center for Responsive Politics. And more than half was injected into Washington's veins in just two critical election cycles: 1999–2000 and 2001–2002. In addition, the industry—led by its trade group, the Pharmaceutical Research and Manufacturers of America (PhRMA)—pours

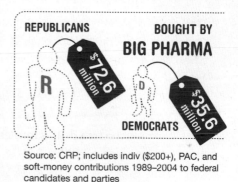

Source: CRP; includes indiv ($200+), PAC, and soft-money contributions 1989–2004 to federal candidates and parties

hundreds of millions into lobbying, employing at least 675 lobbyists. That is more than one for every member of Congress. And it spends tens of millions more on broadcast advertising, much of it through front groups called "Citizens for Better Medicare" and the "United Seniors Association."

Why the huge investment in Washington by Big Pharma in recent years? The industry could see the writing on the wall. The companies' monopoly patents on lucrative medications have been running out (despite numerous valuable extensions granted by Congress), and makers of generic drugs are slowly eating into their markets. Worse yet, years of overcharging American consumers for name-brand drugs have been generating a political backlash.

Starting in the late 1990s, when Congress set up a blue-ribbon commission to study the issue, it was clear that some kind of change was coming.

At Bristol-Myers Squibb, one of the biggest drug companies, top executives were urged to give money to George W. Bush's 2000 campaign. High-level employees were pressured to give the maximum (which was then $1,000 in their own names and $1,000 from their spouses) and warned if they didn't that the company's CEO would be informed, the *New York Times* revealed. "At some companies, officials circulated a videotape of Vice President Al Gore railing against the high price of prescription drugs," the paper reported. The resulting outflow of money—$26.7 million in 2000 and $29.4 million in 2002, tilted even more heavily than usual toward Republicans—was crucial to cementing one-party control of Congress.

One drug lobbyist later crowed in delight, "Having both houses of Congress Republican-controlled was great. Like in Monopoly, when you get to add hotels."

Of course, owners of hotels on Boardwalk and Park Place don't get to charge whatever they want. But that's what industry executives were focused on at a "strategic planning retreat" a few weeks after the November 2002 election. Attendees included Raymond Gilmartin, Merck's chairman ($119,000 personally given since 1999), Sidney Taurel, chairman of Eli Lilly ($69,143), Peter Dolan, chairman of Bristol-Myers Squibb ($43,203) and Robert Essner, president of Wyeth ($26,000). Their four companies alone contributed over $10 million from 1999 onward. One unnamed executive at the retreat told the *Times*, "Sure, we will have more access. Our hand is stronger because of the election results, but who knows how much stronger it really is."

Talk about being disingenuous!

When the dust cleared on the Medicare Prescription Drug, Improvement, and Modernization Act of 2003, a massive bill that set aside $400 billion to supposedly give seniors access to affordable medications, there was one big winner—and her name wasn't Mary Fallacaro.

Even though Americans pay the highest prices in the industrialized world for prescription drugs, Congress did nothing to restrain drug-makers' overall price gouging.

The legislation expressly prohibits Medicare from negotiating lower prices with drug companies (which the Veterans Administration does on behalf of millions of ex-military servicemen and -women to great savings). And the bill does nothing to make it easier for Americans to import cheaper prescription drugs from overseas. Laughably, it insisted that no drug imports even be allowed from Canada, supposedly because of the health dangers to Americans who might buy untested medications from our neighbor to the north.

The correlation between pharmaceutical company campaign

YOUR TAXES PAID TO HELP DEVELOP THESE DRUGS.
BUT WHEN YOU NEED THEM, YOU'LL STILL PAY PREMIUM PRICES!

	AZT	Capoten	Prozac
SUBSIDIZED DRUG	(AIDS treatment) as part of Trizivir	(blood pressure)	(depression)
DRUG SALES	**$287 million** in 2002 for GlaxoSmithKline	**$8 billion** 1996–2002 for Bristol-Myers Squibb	**$392 million** in 2002 for Eli Lilly
CAMPAIGN CONTRIBUTIONS* 1989–2004	**$6.6 million** REPUBLICANS: 76% DEMOCRATS: 23%	**$6.3 million** REPUBLICANS: 81% DEMOCRATS: 19%	**$6.3 million** REPUBLICANS: 75% DEMOCRATS: 25%
DRUG PRICES	$129 Canada $217 U.S.	$47 Canada $118 U.S.	$127 Canada $383 U.S.

*CRP; includes indiv ($200+), PAC, and soft-money contributions to federal candidates and parties
Sources: pharmacy Web sites accessed 4/14/04, Congressional Joint Economic Committee

contributions and votes was crystal clear. In the House of Representatives, for example, the 220 members who voted for the bill received, on average, more than twice as much from pharmaceuticals between 1999 and 2003 as the 215 members who voted against it. Senators who sided with the industry raised 72 percent more campaign cash from Big Pharma than those who voted against the bill.

THEY GAVE MONEY. THEY GOT VOTES. COINCIDENCE?

THE PHARMACEUTICAL INDUSTRY WANTED NO PRICE CONTROLS ON PRESCRIPTION DRUG SUBSIDIES FOR SENIORS*

Senators who said:
SURE! got **$52,000**[†]

House members who said:
SURE! got **$27,600**[†]

Senators who said:
NOPE! got **$30,300**[†]

House members who said:
NOPE! got **$11,300**[†]

*108th Congress, 1st Session, House Vote #669, 220Y-215N; Senate Vote #459, 54Y-44N.
 Y=Industry position †Source: CRP; averages include indiv ($200+) and PAC contributions 1999–2003

And talk about return on investment! The lion's share of the Medicare bill's $400 billion price tag will go into Big Pharma's pockets. The Health Reform Program of Boston University estimated that drug companies will garner $139 billion in increased profits over the program's lifetime of eight years, the equivalent of a 38 percent increase in annual profits for what is already the world's most profitable industry. And that's after you subtract the reductions to profits resulting from Congress's subsidy of private HMOs to compete with Medicare and thus drive down drug prices. (Chances are the pharmaceuticals will make even more, as the White House has since admitted—after the bill had already passed—that it seriously underestimated its total costs, by perhaps as much as another $140 billion!)

This stunning allocation of resources explains why the prescription drug benefit in the bill is so skimpy and full of holes. Once the new program goes into effect in 2006, seniors will get partial coverage for their drug costs. First they have to pay a monthly premium of about $35. Then they have to spend at least $250 of their own money to meet the program's deductible. After that, they get 75 percent of the cost covered on their next $2,250 in prescriptions. Do the math, and you discover that this means seniors will be spending $1,345 out of their own pockets to obtain a hypothetical $2,500 worth of medications. And then the program has what its framers charmingly call a "donut hole"—for it offers no further coverage until a person pays another $2,850 out of their own savings. Only then do relatively generous provisions take hold for catastrophic needs.

The program does give breaks to seniors living close to the poverty line, but a person with as little as $6,000 in assets could be disqualified, leaving out as many as 2.8 million people, according to Families USA, a consumer group.

That's not all. The new law will undermine Medicare by shifting wealthy and healthy people out of its insurance pool into private plans, leaving the taxpayers to pay for the sickest and the poorest among us. Why did Congress choose to take that approach? The insurance industry, source of $95.4 million in campaign cash since 1999, pushed for a new $6.8 billion shelter for tax-free health accounts that will lure wealthy people out of Medicare, while HMOs, the source of $19.6 million since 1999, stand to get $12 billion in tax dollars to skim healthier people out of the program.

* * * * *

"Mr. Chairman, the drug companies are now free, after getting taxpayers' money to develop their product, to gouge those very same people 10, 20 times the cost of their own product. They charge that to the American people who are paying for their research. The American people end up paying twice. Now, is that not nice? This is a corporate form of welfare, and it has got to stop. . . . This is welfare for the rich, for the corporations."

—Representative Dana Rohrabacher (R-CA), July 11, 1996, expressing support for Representative Bernie Sanders's (I-VT) amendment to force companies to reasonably price drugs developed at taxpayer expense. Though the House backed Sanders's proposal in 2000 and 2001, it has never cleared the Senate.

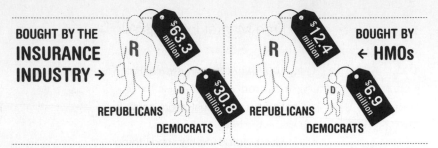

BOUGHT BY THE
INSURANCE
INDUSTRY →

R $63.3 million

D $30.8 million

REPUBLICANS

DEMOCRATS

R $12.4 million

BOUGHT BY
← HMOs

D $6.9 million

REPUBLICANS

DEMOCRATS

Source: CRP; includes indiv ($200+), PAC, and soft-money contributions in 1999–2004 to federal candidates and parties

Even doctors got in on the action, despite the fact that they've seen their power and autonomy dwindle with the rise of HMOs and insurance company bureaucrats. As reporter Jonathan Cohn sleuthed out in the *New Republic,* medical providers like the Republicans' plan. "Who can blame them? Buried within the text of the bill is a 1 percent increase in the money Medicare pays physicians—this instead of a 4 percent decrease that the existing formula would have imposed. So the doctors get more money out of a bill that's supposed to be about giving seniors assistance with prescription drugs. Again, not too shabby—although, again, not so surprising given that health professionals donated $42 million in the 2002 elections, two-thirds of it to the Republican majority."

Senator John McCain (R-AZ) deserves the last word. As the bill reached final passage, he commented: "It's like the ancient medieval practice of leeching. Every special interest is attaching itself to this bill and bleeding Medicare dry."

TEST YOUR MONEY-IN-POLITICS IQ

American consumers are not allowed to import which product from overseas in whatever quantity they want?

a. Beer   b. Fruit   c. Wine   d. Clothes   e. Prescription drugs

Answer: e. Under current law, the FDA will not allow Americans to import anything more than a 90-day supply of medications for personal use.

Congress Says No Free Market in Drugs Allowed; Consumers Barred from Canada

In Citrus County, Florida, with one of the largest elderly populations in the state, four "Canadian Meds" stores have the fax numbers for Canadian pharmacies on speed dial, that's how often customers come in seeking cheap medications. Evelyn Freudeman, 78, is saving $560 a year on her blood pressure and thyroid prescriptions by ordering her meds through a reimporter named "Can-Save Rx." In Kentucky, Edward Cox, 76, and his wife, Mary Lou, 71, spend about $1,000 a month on the drugs they need to treat their rheumatoid arthritis, nervo disorders, and allergies. A trip to Canada to buy a three-month supply saved them about $750.

Faced with ever-increasing drug costs, many Americans have been looking north to Canada, where price controls on pharmaceuticals deliver considerable savings. A month's supply of Lipitor, a popular treatment for high cholesterol, costs $110.99 at CVS.com, an American retailer, and just $64.40 at thecanadiandrugstore.com. Prevacid, an ulcer medication, costs $131.99 here versus $61.94 in Canada, a savings of over 50 percent. Synthrold is $16.49 for a month's supply, compared to $5.99 up north.

One health care expert estimated that Americans could have saved a whopping $38.4 billion in 2001 if they had been charged the average prices for brand-name drugs in Canada, a savings of more than one out of every three dollars we spent on medicines that year!

But thanks to the political clout of the pharmaceutical industry, there is no free market for purchasers of prescription drugs. You can shop around for the best price on a car, a house, or a pair of shoes. But if you want to buy drugs sold legally in Canada, which have been certified as safe by the Canadian government, you can't. Even though both the House and the Senate passed measures to liberalize drug reimportation rules, the pharmaceutical lobby managed to get that provision dropped in conference. Exactly how that happened remains a mystery. But we can infer a few things from the makeup of that powerful group of legislators who ultimately decided the final language of the bill:

- **Representative Billy Tauzin, the Louisiana Republican** who was then chairman of the House Energy and Commerce Committee, has claimed that allowing consumers to buy drugs abroad would be "a disaster to the health and safety of Americans." Along with three of the other four House Republicans on the Medicare conference committee, he voted against allowing the reimportation of drugs from Canada. Over his career in Congress, Tauzin has received $272,997 from pharmaceutical makers and related health products companies, the thirteenth highest of all members of the House, according to the Center for Responsive Politics. And that doesn't even include the money he collected for a separate PAC he controls. As this book went to press, he was reported to be on the verge of leaving Congress to take a $2-million-a-year job heading up federal lobbying for guess who? The Pharmaceutical Research and Manufacturers of America (PhRMA).

- **Senator Orrin Hatch, a Utah Republican**, has long been in the pocket of the pharmaceuticals. In June of 2000, he admitted trying to surreptitiously insert a provision into a military appropriations bill that would have extended the monopoly patent on Claritin for three years beyond its 2002 expiration date. This blatant act of protectionism would have earned Schering-Plough, Claritin's maker, an estimated $2.2 billion in additional revenues. Since generic drug makers were prepared to make the same medication for 80 percent less, this would have been a huge rip-off of consumers. Hatch is the number-one lifetime recipient of pharmaceutical manufacturing contributions in the Senate, with $791,793.

- While seven Democrats from the House and Senate were appointed by their party's leaders to the conference committee, only two were allowed to participate in the negotiating over the final bill: **Senator Max Baucus of Montana and Senator John Breaux of Louisiana**. Respectively, they've received $213,292 and $191,349 from the industry sector during their congressional careers.

NICKEL AND DIMED BY CONGRESS

Working Americans haven't gotten an increase in the minimum wage for eight years, and inflation has taken a huge bite out of its value. Huge majorities support a higher minimum wage. But whenever Congress addresses the issue, wealthy special interests demand tens of billions in tax breaks and other subsidies in exchange. The result: the standard of living of millions of working Americans who are just barely getting by is held hostage to big money in politics.

If you make only the minimum wage of $5.15 an hour, life in America is getting harder. In Sarasota, Florida, it can mean living in a homeless shelter. "We have a lot of people making minimum wage or slightly above, and they can't afford the rents," says Tom Treend, director of the town's YMCA Homeless Youth Education program. A worker would need to make at least $13 an hour to afford a two-bedroom apartment there, where rents average $700 a month.

Demand at food banks is rising. In Huntington, West Virginia, social worker Sidney Polan says, "Utility bills are going up. Income is not. We just have a lot of poor people. Many are working part-time, minimum wage jobs and trying to support three or four people."

About 12,000 residents of Delaware subsist on the minimum wage. Some live at the Whatcoat Social Service Agency's 46-bed shelter in Dover. Shelter executive director Ruth Pugh observes of the people she helps, "They think they can make the rent, but they can't. Or the utilities will be more than what they anticipated. And you can only do so much on a $6- or $7-an-hour job."

These are the facts:

Nearly 7 million workers are paid at or below the minimum hourly wage. Almost seven out of ten of them are adults, contrary to the perception that most minimum wage workers are teenagers seeking a little extra income. Nearly half work full time. About one third are parents of children under 18. Four in ten minimum wage workers are the sole source of income for their families. Another 10.5 million workers earn less than a dollar more than the minimum wage.

In the 1960s, the minimum wage was enough to lift a family of three just over the federal poverty level. No longer, thanks to inflation and Congress's increasing reluctance to raise the wage floor.

To reach the federal poverty line for a family of three now ($13,120), the minimum would have to be $6.30 an hour. If the minimum wage in 1968 of $1.60 an hour had been adjusted for inflation to the present, it would have reached $8.46 in 2003, well above the $5.15 level that was set in 1996. Or, to put it another way, taking inflation into account, today's minimum wage is worth almost 25 percent less than what it was worth in 1979.

Americans are not insensitive to the plight of low-wage workers. Polls consistently show that large majorities favor raising the minimum wage. For example, a January 2002 poll by Lake Snell Perry & Associates for the Ms. Foundation found that 77 percent supported raising the wage from $5.15 to $8.00 an hour. An October 2001 poll by Gallup/CNN/USA Today found 81 percent support a general increase in the minimum wage.

But even though hiking the minimum wage is popular, we rarely hear about it in Washington. That's because low-income people can't afford to pay to play. Half or more of the workers in some fifty occupations are paid poverty-level wages. And these folks don't make many campaign contributions. For example, some 3.4 million people make a living as cashiers, but FEC records show only 23 contributions from cashiers reported in the current 2003–2004 election

TOTAL CONTRIBUTIONS BY SELECTED OCCUPATIONS

2004 election cycle*

This chart shows how much people working in different occupations—some high-income, some low-income—have given in itemized campaign contributions, as they reported them to the Federal Election Commission. The contributions were made in the 2004 election cycle and were downloaded by the Center for Responsive Politics from the agency in February 2004. The chart probably undercounts how many contributions people in these lines of work made. While the law requires people making campaign contributions over $200 to record their occupations, many people leave the lines blank. In addition, people don't report their occupation in a consistent fashion; rather, there are many variations: e.g., "C.E.O.," "Chief Executive Officer," "Chief Exec. Ofcr.," etc. For this chart, therefore, we standardized the occupations. The total amounts are also an undercount, since we are including only donors of more than $200 who listed their occupations. We also don't know, of course, what the occupations are of people contributing under $200; however, we do know that the amount of money given in contributions over $200 dwarfs the total given by those under $200. In the last presidential election cycle (2000), $912 million came in the form of contributions over $200, versus $550 million under $200.

Even with these cautionary notes, it's still clear that one group of people is paying to play in politics, and one isn't. The next time you hear a politician brag about how something she just did will help ordinary working people, ask her how many cashiers or janitors or maids have given her a campaign contribution.

DEMOCRATS ■   REPUBLICANS ▓

Occupation	Total
attorney	$49,925,300
executive	$25,180,300
CEO	$18,899,300
doctor	$18,335,300
investor	$7,554,700
lobbyist	$2,510,400
accountant	$1,841,000
marketing	$1,405,500
producer	$1,138,700
actor	$304,300
real estate broker	$270,900
maid/janitor	$31,100
cashier	$13,700
security guard	$7,900
waiter/waitress	$6,000
farm worker	$5,800
taxi/chauffeur	$4,300
manicurist	$4,000
bartender	$3,500
dishwasher	$800

*Source: CRP; indivs ($200+) to federal candidates, leadership PACs, and parties, Public Campaign analysis

cycle. Of the nearly half a million people employed as dishwashers, FEC filings show just one contribution from a donor identified as such. Of the more than two million janitors, maids, and cleaners, whose median income in 2002 of $8.77 an hour was barely enough to lift a family of four out of poverty, just 68 campaign contributions of $200 or more listed that occupation. By comparison, people in high-income occupations like attorneys, doctors, executives, CEOs, and investors riddle the ranks of campaign contributors.

Of course, unions are strong advocates of raising the minimum wage, and they do contribute significant sums, which represent the pooling of millions of very small contributions by their members. But they are vastly outspent by big business. In 2000 and 2002, for example, labor unions contributed just over $187 million, while business interests gave $2.2 billion.

Individual contributions of more than $200 are the single largest source of money in politics—providing about $2.25 billion in the 2000 and 2002 election cycles. Only about 800,000 people make such contributions, about one quarter of one percent of the whole U.S. population. Eighty percent of this elite group make over $100,000 a year.

Unfortunately, this group—which is primarily made up of business owners, high-level executives, lawyers, and lobbyists—isn't

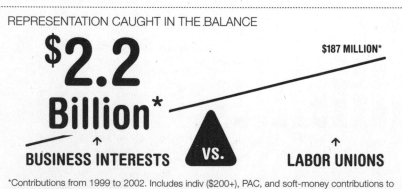

REPRESENTATION CAUGHT IN THE BALANCE

$2.2 Billion*

$187 MILLION*

↑
BUSINESS INTERESTS   VS.   **LABOR UNIONS**

*Contributions from 1999 to 2002. Includes indiv ($200+), PAC, and soft-money contributions to federal candidates and parties.

very interested in raising the minimum wage. And so, whenever legislation to do so has gained enough steam to be voted on in the House or Senate, wealthy special interests that give most of the money for campaigns have demanded all kinds of special favors as the price of allowing a minimum wage increase to pass.

Back in 1996, the last time Congress voted to lift the minimum wage, raising it by 90 cents to $5.15 an hour, business interests extracted almost $30 billion in custom-designed tax benefits as part of the process. While the politicians harped on what they were doing for working people, the fine print actually did a lot more for big business. According to the Center for Responsive Politics, special interests gave more than $36 million in campaign contributions in the previous election cycle to the members of the House

Kids Ask the Darnedest Things

President Bush, who has the power of the "bully pulpit" to put any topic on the national front-burner, doesn't like to talk about the minimum wage much. Indeed, the very term has rarely passed through his lips, according to a search of the White House Web site, which offers extensive transcripts of his public remarks at all sorts of events. The press has never asked him about it either, at any of his infrequent press conferences. Indeed, the only time any member of the public appears to have engaged him in an on-the-record discussion of the topic was back in 1999, when he was governor of Texas and running for president.

Bush was seated in a classroom filled with thirty elementary school children, all African American. He was visiting The Door, a Christian summer program for poor kids in East Baltimore. Most of the kids asked Bush the sorts of questions kids ask: What are your hobbies? Do you have any pets? What college did you go to? Then a little girl piped up and said, "If you become president, are you going to raise the minimum wage?" According to John Judis, a reporter who witnessed the scene, Bush seemed "momentarily taken aback." "That's up to Congress," he replied at first. Then, sensing that he hadn't satisfied the girl, he added, "What I worry about, though, is pricing people out of work." He later said that he was in favor of an increase in the federal minimum wage, as long as states were allowed to opt out of it.

Ways and Means Committee and Senate Finance Committee who drafted the provisions benefiting those industries.

The Small Business Job Protection Act—as the minimum wage bill of 1996 was titled—actually delivered big benefits to many not-so-small businesses. Pharmaceutical companies, high-tech, and soft-drink producers—the source of at least $24 million in contributions in that election cycle—got a loophole in the tax code worth $18 billion over ten years. Members of National Federation of Independent Business (NFIB) got an increase in the deductibility of major equipment purchases, saving them $4.7 billion over ten years. They also got changes in pension laws worth $6 billion. Owners of convenience stores got Congress to reverse an IRS ruling, saving them $452 million.

Three years later, the same dynamic was at work, except that business interests and their congressional allies had gotten bolder—having seen how easy it was to tack their pet proposals onto the highly popular minimum wage issue. At the time, congressional Democrats were urging a $1 increase in the minimum wage, spread over two years.

"Instead of having a spoonful of sugar to help the medicine go down, some of our Members would like a wheelbarrow of sugar," said a spokesman for the powerful House Ways and Means chair, Bill Archer (R-TX).

Thus, a bipartisan group of House members proposed $35 billion in sweet business tax breaks, while spreading out the $1 increase in the minimum wage over three years. They had a dollop for the restaurant and hotel industry, which had invested $10.8 million in campaign contributions in the 1997–1998 cycle: an increase in the business meal tax deduction—bring back the three-martini lunch!—that would have cost the taxpayers $11.6 billion over the next ten years. Other sweeteners included an increase in tax credits aimed at helping businesses hire entry-level workers (cost: $2 billion over five years), and full deductibility for small businesses' health care expenses (cost: $3 billion over five years). Ultimately the $1 increase was attached to a House bill containing

$240 billion in tax cuts. This bill hit a logjam in the Senate, which had chosen the more "moderate" tack of seeking only $75 billion in tax breaks, while spreading the $1 wage increase out over three years; that is, 33 cents for some, $75 billion for others. Even though both chambers of Congress passed versions of the idea, they were never reconciled. Special interest greed ended up defeating another increase in the minimum wage.

* * * * *

"You're either on the outside or the inside, and the only thing that can get you on the inside is money."

—*Former Representative Joe Scarborough (R-FL), quoted in* Speaking Freely, 2nd edition, CRP

The election of President George W. Bush hasn't stopped advocates from pushing for another increase in the wage floor. But they have become resigned to the price they have to be willing to pay special interests in order to help average working people. In May of 2002, Senator Ted Kennedy (D-MA), who has been pushing to raise the minimum $1.50 over three years, said that he'd be willing to accept business tax cuts worth anywhere from $20 to $30 billion if that's what it takes. Emboldened by their success at winning all kinds of tax breaks since the Republican takeover of the White House and Congress, a coalition of business groups asked members to reject Kennedy's feeler. The minimum wage increase was dead again.

MONOPOLY IS SO MUCH FUN

Eight years after Congress deregulated the communications marketplace, amid promises of increased competition and lowered prices, consumers are being hit year after year by outrageous increases in their cable TV bills. While prices for all kinds of other commodities have dropped, the cable industry has figured out how to keep its monopoly untouched: Buy Congress.

In 1997, a top-of-the-line home PC (with a Pentium II processor, 32 megabytes of RAM, a 19-inch monitor, and an 8.5-gigabyte hard drive) cost $2,900. Seven years later, a PC with far more storage capacity and speed (a Pentium IV processor, 512 megabytes of RAM, a 19-inch flat panel display, and a 160-gigabyte hard drive) goes for $1,999. Plus you can get a DVD/CD read-write recorder at no extra cost.

That's not the only major commodity that's gone down in price in the last few years. The cost of furniture and bedding dropped almost 4 percent between 1997 and 2003, according to the Labor Department's Bureau of Labor Statistics. A new car? Down almost 4.5 percent. Audio equipment? Down 20 percent. A television? Down a whopping 41 percent! In general, personal computers and peripherals are down a stunning 80 percent in price.

While prices for many products have dropped in recent years, there are a few basic commodities whose prices have risen far faster than the general rise in the cost of living, which has gone up just 12 percent from 1997 to 2003. The price of prescription drugs, which we covered in Chapter 1, has become a major issue. That's not a surprise when you consider that they've risen 31 percent in price since 1997. Another commodity whose price has soared—but one that has gotten almost no attention in Congress—is cable TV.

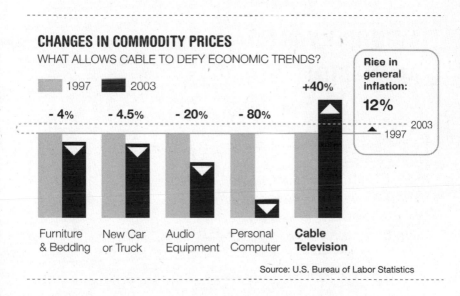

CHANGES IN COMMODITY PRICES
WHAT ALLOWS CABLE TO DEFY ECONOMIC TRENDS?

■ 1997   ■ 2003

+40%

Rise in general inflation: 12%

- 4%   - 4.5%   - 20%   - 80%

2003
1997

Furniture & Bedding | New Car or Truck | Audio Equipment | Personal Computer | **Cable Television**

Source: U.S. Bureau of Labor Statistics

Since 1997 the average monthly bill for basic cable has gone from $26.06 to $36.47. That's a 40 percent increase, or an extra $125 a year. Considering that over 70 million American households get TV service from a cable operator, that means the industry is raking in a cool $8 billion to $9 billion per year more than it did just a few years ago, while providing little improvement, if any, in services.

In some places, the rise in prices has been unbelievable. Cablevision subscribers in New York City, for example, have seen their bills go up 94 percent since 1997.

How do the cable companies get away with raising their prices, year after year? A one-word answer will suffice: Monopoly.

The cable industry is "one of the most persistent monopolies in the American economy," said Joel Klein, the then-head of the Justice Department's Antitrust Division, in May 1998.

Wait a second. What about the Telecommunications Act of 1996? The bill's sponsors promised that the landmark legislation, which ended most government regulation of the communications marketplace, would usher in a new age of competition between telephone, cable, and broadcast companies, bringing new choices and lower rates for America's consumers.

Well, it hasn't worked out that way. A recent study of industry competition conducted by the U.S. General Accounting Office found that only 2 percent of all markets offered a choice of two or more cable providers. In those few places, rates are about 15 percent lower, on average. Direct broadcast satellite services like DirecTV and EchoStar reach about 18 million households, but that competition has made only a tiny dent in cable rates, amounting to about 15 cents a month. Everywhere else, the situation is reminiscent of the code of honor between thieves, that is, you never steal from another thief.

Three years after the Telecommunications Act became law, the Consumer Federation of America and Consumers Union reported that instead of attacking each other's markets, local cable and telephone monopolies had focused on merging into "larger and larger regional firms that now form tight national oligopolies." The groups issued that report hoping to convince Congress to revisit a provision of the Telecommunications Act that formally ended price controls on cable services by March 31, 1999. But their study fell on deaf ears.

No wonder. The communications and electronics sector invested heavily in the passage of the Telecommunications Act, donating $60.6 million to federal candidates and parties in 1995–1996

> * * * * *
>
> *"I was trapped in five to eight fund-raisers, quite often, per day. I was also a sitting member of Congress, so we'd be on our way to a fund-raiser and a vote that we thought wasn't going to happen would happen, and I'd have to turn around and jump on a plane for Washington."*
>
> —Former **Representative Rick Lazio** (R-NY), Speaking Freely, 2nd edition, CRP

alone. The cable industry, a smaller but by no means insignificant subset of that group, has fought hard to keep Congress and the regulatory agencies from reviewing the law, giving $20.3 million since then. The lead sponsor of the Telecommunications Act, Senator Larry

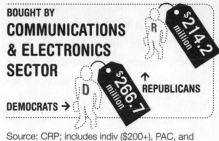

BOUGHT BY
COMMUNICATIONS & ELECTRONICS SECTOR
DEMOCRATS →
D $266.7 million
R $214.2 million
↑ REPUBLICANS

Source: CRP; includes indiv ($200+), PAC, and soft-money contributions 1989–2004 to federal candidates and parties

Pressler (R-SD), was the top overall recipient of cable industry cash, with $117,299.

In the summer of 1998 the Senate killed a proposal that would have simply asked the FCC to study rising cable rates. On average, senators voting against the proposal got 21 percent more in contributions over the previous six years from cable PACs and individuals who work in the industry than did senators who voted in favor. A February 1998 bill sponsored by Representative Edward Markey (D-MA), a longtime consumer advocate in Congress, that would have kept price controls on cable services in place after March 1999, was buried by the House Commerce subcommittee on telecommunications, trade, and consumer protection. Subcommittee members received, on average, twice as much as the average House member in contributions from the cable guys during the 1997–1998 election cycle.

The cable companies defend their price increases by claiming that they have to pay more for programming, and by arguing that they need higher profits to pay for capital expenditures on system upgrades. In fact, the Consumer Federation of America points out, cable operators actually own a lot of programming, which means rising prices for things like sporting events just shift money from one subdivision of a cable company to another—either way consumers are still paying them more. And between 1998 and 2001, cable companies spent over a quarter-trillion dollars gobbling each other up, six times as much as their spending on capital upgrades.

The cable companies also argue that their higher prices are justified in part because they're offering more channels to subscribers as part of their basic services. But the Bureau of Labor Statistics says that even after they account for that improvement, cable rates have risen at three times the rate of inflation. The truth is most cable customers are paying for far more channels than they regularly watch. And they don't have much choice in the matter.

Why doesn't anyone protest? Consumer groups say the public has given up on complaining about rising cable rates because they have no hope of winning changes in today's Washington. As Representative Markey recently told the *New York Times,* "They can't go to the House, they can't go to the Senate, and they can't go to the president, because nobody cares."

WHEN BIG BANKS HAPPEN TO LITTLE PEOPLE (PART 1)

Big money in politics won one of its biggest victories ever in 1999 when Congress repealed a Depression-era law preventing banks, securities firms, and insurance companies from merging and getting into each other's business. The meltdown of the telecom market in 2002 may be only a taste of things to come.

Were you an investor in WorldCom, the once-high-flying telecommunications giant that went bankrupt in the summer of 2002 after the world learned it had inflated its earnings by $9 billion? Have you lost money in the $2 trillion (that's $2,000,000,000,000) collapse of the telecommunications bubble that has taken place since then? Were you someone who listened to stock market analysts who pumped these stocks—people like Henry Blodget and Jack Grubman—working for Merrill Lynch, Goldman Sachs, J. P. Morgan, or any of seven other name-brand Wall Street firms who, in April 2003, paid nearly a half billion dollars in fines and another $900 million in other penalties for years of misleading investors?

Have you noticed that charges for checking accounts and other banking services seem to have taken off in recent years?

If so, then count yourself a victim of one of the greatest victories of big money in politics ever—one in which close to three-quarters of a billion dollars were spent on campaign contributions and lobbying. Hold on to your seats, because the way we came to this pass is quite a tale—and not one that's been told much by the big media conglomerates.

Friday, October 22, 1999, should be remembered as an infamous day in our country's history. That was the day that White House and Senate negotiators worked out a final, late-night deal engineering the repeal of a critical Depression-era law, the Glass-Steagall Act, that for close to six decades kept the banking, securities, and insurance businesses separate from each other. Born out of the lessons of the 1929 market crash, the law, which was named for its sponsors Senator Carter Glass (D-VA) and Representative Henry Steagall (D-AL), had forced commercial banks to choose between the relatively conservative business of holding individual deposits and lending money, or the riskier world of underwriting securities. The law also set up the Federal Deposit Insurance Corporation (FDIC) to protect individuals from losing their life savings in the event of a bank failure.

Starting in the 1960s, banks started lobbying Congress to loosen these restrictions. The pace of their demands rose in the 1970s as securities firms began nibbling on their territory by offering interest-paying money-market accounts—albeit without deposit insurance—and other traditional bank services like check writing. Then the floodgates opened in the mid-1980s, as the Federal Reserve began reinterpreting sections of Glass-Steagall to allow banks into the securities business, albeit to a limited degree.

As regulators loosened the rules, the whole array of interests affected—large and small banks, insurance companies, and securities firms—turned to Congress to rewrite the law. Former Securities and Exchange Commission chairman Arthur Levitt described the scene to PBS's *Frontline* program, which aired a noteworthy exposé in the spring of 2003:

> During a period of time when [Senator] Al D'Amato (R-NY) chaired the [Senate] Banking Committee—and was not successful in getting the repeal of Glass-Steagall . . . hundreds of lobbyists descended upon the Congress, were in there always morning, day and night. Lobbyists for the insurance companies, for the investment banks, for the commercial banks, pulling

for their own parochial interests. Then when [Senator] Phil Gramm (R-TX) became chairman of the banking committee, the same group came down, only they were now supplemented by lobbyists for the derivatives industry, for other new products that had developed, and for the exchanges and the options exchanges. They were buttonholing senators and congressmen, morning, day, and night.

But for years, conflicts between these sectors prevented the passage of a bill as they fenced over its provisions. Key members of the House and Senate Banking Committees made out like bandits: Senator D'Amato received $7 million from the financial sector, ranking him number 3 lifetime among all senators. Senator Gramm took in $5.5 million, ranking number 5 lifetime. On the House side, Representative Bill McCollum (R-FL) raised $2.3 million, putting him at number 5 lifetime and Representative Michael Oxley (R-OH) raised $2.0 million, number 11 lifetime. To some observers, the giant fight over the terms of deregulating the banking and securities businesses seemed like the perfect cash cow for incumbent members of Congress—one they could milk every two years by promising to pass legislation, only to blame failure on competing interests and then start the whole extortion process again in the next congressional cycle.

All that finally changed in early 1998, when Sandy Weill, the acquisitive head of the Travelers insurance company (which had recently gobbled up the Salomon Brothers investment bank, forming Salomon Smith Barney) struck a deal with John Reed of Citicorp (parent of Citibank) to merge their two firms. The $70 billion stock swap they announced on April 6, 1998, to create Citigroup Inc. was then the largest corporate merger in history. But they had one problem: unless Congress changed the law, Citigroup would eventually be forced to shed its insurance business. Technically, the merger was illegal when it was announced, but that didn't stop the financial titans.

Weill's lobbying campaign started with a phone call to then–treasury secretary Robert Rubin. When Weill said he had important news,

Rubin quipped, "You're buying the government?" The joke wasn't far from the truth.

According to Charles Geisst, a professor of finance and author of many books on Wall Street, the push from Citigroup was so persistent that on Capitol Hill the bill to repeal Glass-Steagall, the Financial Services Modernization Act, "was referred to as 'the Citi-Travelers Act.'" He told *Frontline* that in 1998, the year before the bill was passed, Citigroup spent $100 million on lobbying and public relations alone, and other financial firms threw in a similar amount.

Of course, that wasn't all. Between 1997 and 2000, the finance, insurance, and real estate sector (which includes commercial banking and securities and investment firms) poured over $456 million into the pockets of federal candidates and parties, 60 percent to Republicans and 40 percent to Democrats. Citigroup alone gave nearly $7 million. Some of its contributions came at crucial moments. In early May 1999, on the very day the Senate voted to approve the bill, Citigroup tossed $55,000 in soft money to two Republican party committees, according to the Center for Responsive Politics. And a month later, as the House took up the bill, the company gave $50,000 to the Democratic Congressional Campaign Committee. Political ideology didn't matter to Citigroup: it made sure to buy access and influence with all sides. (And Robert Rubin went to work as Weill's top lieutenant days after the bill became law.)

Under the provisions of the Financial Services Modernization Act, insurance companies, brokerage houses, banks, and credit card companies were freed to merge with each other. Proponents said the law was needed to allow American banks to compete with superlarge foreign banks that did not operate under the same restrictions. They also claimed that the new megabanks would become convenient "one-stop-shopping" financial supermarkets and that this would save consumers billions in lower loan rates and banking fees. They promised that a "Chinese wall" would divide the megabanks' commercial and securities arms, and no conflicts of interest would arise.

Opponents warned that allowing these megamergers would lead to a dangerous concentration of power, with banks risking depositors' funds on dicey loans offered to companies whose stocks they were promoting, or with banks plumping for stocks of companies they were in bed with. They feared that not only would small investors get trampled in the process, but ultimately taxpayers could be left paying the costs if a megabank's risky business ventures led to its failure. As top regulator Arthur Levitt described it to *Frontline*:

> Let's say that a commercial bank underwrites a company. Millions of shares are outstanding in the public's hands, and the company's fortunes sink. Ordinarily, that commercial bank would place the interests of their depositors above all others at that point, and if the loan didn't make sense, they'd call the loan, or they wouldn't give them additional funds. What kind of judgment are they going to make at this point, where they have perhaps a million investors out there who have bought shares in the company that their name is on? They will probably go a step further and lend more money and more money. . . . Then we have the shareholders in the bank and the depositors in the bank at risk.

We now know that the critics were right, and that the deregulation of the banking and securities industries let loose a wave of dangerous financial hankypanky.

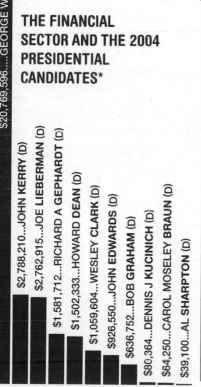

THE FINANCIAL SECTOR AND THE 2004 PRESIDENTIAL CANDIDATES*

$20,769,596.....GEORGE W BUSH (R)

$2,788,210...JOHN KERRY (D)

$2,762,915...JOE LIEBERMAN (D)

$1,581,712...RICHARD A GEPHARDT (D)

$1,502,333...HOWARD DEAN (D)

$1,059,604...WESLEY CLARK (D)

$926,550...JOHN EDWARDS (D)

$636,752...BOB GRAHAM (D)

$80,364...DENNIS J KUCINICH (D)

$64,250...CAROL MOSELEY BRAUN (D)

$39,100...AL SHARPTON (D)

*Includes indiv ($200+) and PAC contributions

"The repeal of Glass-Steagall was an accelerator for the telecom bubble, because remember, telecom companies need to raise an enormous amount of capital," says Scott Cleland, the founder and CEO of the Precursor Group, a research outfit that provides expert advice on the telecom industry to institutional investors. "These Glass-Steagall-enabled companies were able to provide whatever capital a telecom company could ever hope to raise."

WorldCom was the telecom bubble's most spectacular failure, and it couldn't have happened without Citigroup. *Frontline*'s Hedrick Smith found that:

- "Citigroup curried favor with WorldCom and its CEO, Bernie Ebbers, by providing excessively positive ratings of WorldCom shares by Salomon Smith Barney's telecom analyst Jack Grubman."
- When WorldCom was starting to sink and looking for investment banks to help it float a $17 billion debt offering, Citigroup used its Travelers insurance arm to issue a $1 billion personal mortgage to Ebbers, which he used to start cashing out his WorldCom wealth without selling his shares, which would have triggered warning sirens on Wall Street. (Ebbers was indicted on securities fraud in early 2004.)
- Citigroup accepted WorldCom stock as collateral for that loan to Ebbers, which gave it an additional interest in Jack Grubman's issuing analyst reports telling investors to buy the stock.
- Internal e-mails obtained by regulators show that Grubman was aware of accounting irregularities at WorldCom, but instead of reporting them, he coached company executives on what to tell other stock analysts so they wouldn't find out.
- None of these interrelationships were disclosed to individual investors by Salomon Smith Barney, which was selling them WorldCom stocks and bonds.

The Worldcom implosion was just one of many Wall Street scandals that made headlines in the first years of the new century. Investigations spurred by New York attorney general Eliot Spitzer ultimately unveiled systemic conflicts of interest throughout the industry. One recurring theme: stock analysts in one arm of a firm would talk up a stock, often one they knew was weak, while another arm was making a killing selling it. Spitzer blames the repeal of Glass-Steagall for the explosion of corruption. "There is no question that we have created a web of relationships that provide the opportunity for massive abuse. And what we uncovered . . . demonstrates there was massive abuse."

In the spring of 2003 Spitzer and federal regulators announced a global settlement with ten top firms, fining them $1.4 billion for their behavior, but indicting no one for any crimes. High-flying analysts Blodget and Grubman were also fined millions and barred

Fleecing the Little People

Proponents of the Financial Services Modernization Act predicted that the mergers it would allow could save consumers $15 billion a year in lower rates and fees. It hasn't turned out that way. According to a 2003 survey by Bankrate.com, punitive fees and checking account costs are siphoning increasing amounts of money out of consumers' accounts. Bounced check fees are up 20 percent from 1998. The minimum amount required in an account to avoid monthly service fees averaging nearly $11 is up more than 44 percent, to over $2,250. This isn't a trivial matter to the more than 12 million families who don't have enough money to even open a bank account, or the 48 million households that keep $1,000 or less in their accounts. Consumers Union has also found that larger banks tend to charge noncustomers much higher check-cashing fees than smaller and regional banks. In general, says the Bureau of Labor Statistics, the average cost of checking accounts and other banking services has increased 19 percent between 1998 and 2003.

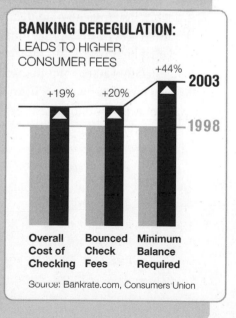

BANKING DEREGULATION:
LEADS TO HIGHER CONSUMER FEES

+19% +20% +44%

2003

1998

| Overall Cost of Checking | Bounced Check Fees | Minimum Balance Required |

Source: Bankrate.com, Consumers Union

for life from the securities business. For Wall Street, these costs were a slap on the wrist—"symbolic," in the words of Arthur Levitt (who was chairman of the American Stock Exchange before going into government). The firms also promised to physically separate their stock research and investment

BOUGHT BY THE FINANCIAL SECTOR

Source: CRP; includes indiv ($200+), PAC, and soft-money contributions 1989–2004 to federal candidates and parties

banking departments to prevent the exchange of information between divisions and promised to stop giving away lucrative initial public offerings to CEOs.

But veteran Wall Street observers say little has been done to fix the underlying problems. As telecom analyst Scott Cleland put it, "The 'Chinese wall' was a joke. It turned out to be a Chinese shower curtain. That is because you have people that are literally in the same room, or one or two walls apart, who are trying to keep things separate, when the financial incentive is to bring them together." Attorney General Spitzer, who favors the breakup of the megabanks, says he doesn't see "any evidence in Washington that there is a will to do so."

It will probably take more spectacular stock market failures, with millions of innocent investors burned and thousands of hardworking people thrown out of work, before anything starts to change.

HOW CONGRESS UNLEASHED THE LOOTERS

If "bipartisan" means "buy one party and get the other one free," that was never truer than in the way big money from the securities, accounting, and high-tech industries bought Congress in the 1990s and got the feds to drastically loosen the rules governing the stock market and the accounting industry. The painful result: millions of us are deferring our retirements and wondering whether we can trust the markets. Maybe the correct spelling of the word should be "buy-partisan."

Paul Palombo is a long-distance truck driver. He turned 63 last year. Like many Americans, he started contributing to a 401(k) in 1982 and did a good job investing his savings. "I got in when the getting was good, and it grew from zero to almost $250,000," he told Christine Dugas of *USA Today*. "I said, 'This is great! I can retire at 55.'"

But the deep drop in the markets that occurred in the wake of widespread accounting scandals at firms like Enron, Global Crossing, Tyco, WorldCom, and Adelphia—which produced a cumulative drop of about $7 trillion in market value following a high of $17 trillion—hit Palombo hard, costing him $50,000 in 2002 alone and leaving him wondering when, if ever, he'd be able to retire.

Palombo is not alone. Like two-thirds of American adults, he has been saving for his retirement in part by investing in 401(k)s or

IRAs. According to a 2002 Gallup poll taken during the worst downturn in the market, nearly half of those people said they will need to postpone that happy day because of their losses in the stock market. And lots of people—44 percent according to the survey—said they're expecting to live less comfortably when they do retire. More recent surveys show that little has improved. A September 2003 survey done by Harris Interactive for Allstate found that 3 out of 10 Americans expected they would have to delay their retirement by an average of almost six years.

Investing has always involved risk. But ever since the Great Crash of 1929 and the creation of the Securities and Exchange Commission (SEC) to regulate the markets, Americans have properly expected that, as the SEC states on its Web site, "Companies publicly offering securities for investment dollars must tell the public the truth about their businesses, the securities they are selling, and the risks involved in investing" and "people who sell and trade securities—brokers, dealers and exchanges—must treat investors fairly and honestly, putting investors' interests first."

Those assumptions were shattered by the corporate scandals at Enron and Arthur Andersen, where company executives played fast and loose with the books, and the accountants—supposedly independent auditors whose job was to certify to the public the accountability of those corporate statements—were in on the scams. Ultimately, more than 700 U.S. companies have been forced to admit filing misleading financial statements, at a cost to investors of an estimated $200 billion.

None of this could have happened without the help of Congress, acting in thrall to big money from the securities, high-tech, and accounting industries.

The first reckless change made by Congress was the treatment of stock options. Back in 1994, the Financial Accounting Standards Board (FASB) was preparing to rule that the granting of such options be treated as a company expense. That step would have reduced corporate earnings and thus deflated stock values. But it would have also tempered the rise in CEO pay and it would have reduced the incentive for CEOs to artificially inflate their company's stock price through all sorts of deceptive accounting schemes. However, most CEOs simply saw the proposed change as an attack on their compensation, and convinced lawmakers that it would stifle incentives. In response, the Senate passed a nonbinding resolution sponsored by Senator Joe Lieberman (D-CT) calling on the FASB to back down, which it did.

Arthur Levitt was chairman of the SEC then, and he later told the PBS program *Frontline*, "There was no question in my mind that campaign contributions played the determinative role in the Senate activity."

The high-tech (computers and Internet companies) and securities industries, which pushed hard to protect stock options from being expensed, have poured $432 million into congressional coffers since 1989. Lieberman ranks high as a beneficiary of their largesse: over his lifetime he is number 7 among his Senate colleagues in receiving contributions from the securities and investment industry, having collected $1.5 million, and he has gotten more than $322,000 from the computer industry, seventh among all Senators.

BOUGHT BY
HIGH-TECH &
SECURITIES
INDUSTRIES

DEMOCRATS
$203.2 million

REPUBLICANS
$226.9 million

Source: CRP; includes indiv ($200+), PAC, and soft-money contributions 1989–2004 to federal candidates and parties

Sarah Teslik, the executive director of the Council of Institutional Investors, a group that represents pension funds, told *Frontline,* "Had FASB changed the rules and required companies to show stock options as an expense, I think Enron and a number of the other companies that have tanked through fraudulent bookkeeping would have been held back considerably." She recalls the lobbying onslaught to prevent the change:

"You had groups, mainstream business lobbies; you had the Silicon Valley lobbies; you had the accountants . . . all calling on every senator and congressman, leaning on the SEC . . .

kicking in large campaign contributions. It was one of the most impressive lobbying efforts on earth. It was protecting CEOs' pay packages. . . . I mean, there's nothing in CEOs' salaries that compares to the number of CEO stock options. It was protecting CEOs' pay packages. They were out in force."

The ability of companies to dispense options without having to account for them led to an explosion in executive compensation and gave top corporate officials a big incentive to artificially inflate their stock prices. You might think that after the Enron and Arthur Andersen scandals, the idea of expensing stock options might seem like common sense. But while Congress was debating corporate reform in the summer of 2002, Senate Majority Leader Tom Daschle (D-SD) twice used parliamentary rules to block a vote on a proposal to force companies to count them as a real expense. Stock options proponents like Lieberman and Silicon Valley venture capitalist John Doerr, who with his wife, Anne, has given $743,000 to the Democratic Party and its candidates since 1999, according to the Center for Responsive Politics, claim that millions of workers benefit from "owning a piece of the company." In fact, according to the National Center for Employee Ownership, the top five executives of most companies held 75 percent of all options outstanding in 2000, with the next fifty executives holding another 15 percent. Only 1.5 percent of all nonexecutive employees earning between $35,000 and $50,000 in 1999 had any stock options, and usually the number of shares involved is minuscule.

Another legislative decision that helped unleash the corporate looters came in December 1995, when Congress overrode President Clinton's veto of a bill that made it harder for shareholders to file and win lawsuits against company officials or accountants, and made it easier for top executives to get away scot-free with making slippery financial projections. The bill, known as the Private Securities Litigation Reform Act, came to the fore as part of Newt Gingrich's Contract With America, but it had bipartisan support, especially from Democratic senator Christopher Dodd of Connecticut, who was then also the chairman of the Democratic National Committee. Among the law's major provisions: companies would be shielded from liability for making overly optimistic "forward looking statements" in their pitches to potential investors. In other words, a company could make all sorts of claims about its rosy future, and, as long as it included a blanket disclaimer along with the statement, it couldn't be held liable. Accountants were perhaps the biggest winners in the law, beating back an attempt to reinstate liability for those who "aid and abet" securities fraud.

The law's supporters said it would cut down on frivolous securities lawsuits. But a long list of consumer and state and municipal groups lobbied against the legislation, arguing that it would make it more difficult for the victims of fraud to recover their losses—thus emboldening corporate shysters. When President Clinton, under pressure from trial lawyers, generous campaign contributors in their own right, vetoed the bill, Dodd helped organize the

BOUGHT BY

ACCOUNTING INDUSTRY

DEMOCRATS

$29.4 million

$43.5 million

REPUBLICANS

Source: CRP; includes indiv ($200+), PAC, and soft-money contributions 1989–2004 to federal candidates and parties

Senate to override his veto, 68 to 30. Even though he wasn't up for reelection in 1996, Dodd received $555,000 from the securities, accounting, and computer industries that pushed for securities litigation reform. He has raised more than $2.6 million over his lifetime in office from these industries. Then–Speaker of the House Gingrich raised $289,000 from those sectors in 1996 alone.

The last deregulatory fight that unleashed the corporate looters was the all-out effort by the accounting industry in 1999 and 2000 to prevent the SEC from forcing accountants to stop selling consulting services to the same companies that they audited—an obvious conflict of interest, we now know in hindsight. (At the same time that Arthur Andersen was making $25 million a year auditing Enron's books, it was raking in an additional $27 million consulting for the company.) Forty-seven senators and representatives wrote Arthur Levitt, who was still then the SEC's chairman, and successfully forced him to back down. These members of Congress were on average the recipients of $93,000 each from the Big Five accounting firms and the industry trade association, the American Institute of Certified Public Accountants. Overall the accounting industry has given $73.3 million to federal candidates and parties since 1989.

"They waged a war against us, a total war," Levitt later told *New Yorker* **magazine. "If there was ever an example where money and lobbying damaged the public interest, this was clearly it. . . . It used to be that if industries had a problem they would try to work it out with the regulatory authorities. Now they bypass the regulators completely and go to Congress. It's almost impossible to compete with the effect that money has on these congressmen."**

Representative Billy Tauzin (R-LA), then the powerful chairman of the House Energy and Commerce Committee, was one of Levitt's chief nemeses. Not only did he write Levitt a four-page single-spaced letter asking the SEC chairman a series of very pointed questions, he threatened to cut the regulatory agency's funding if Levitt went through with his plan to separate auditing and consulting services. He "badgered me relentlessly," Levitt recalled. "He knew what the accountants were doing before I did. He was working very closely with them. I don't mean to sound cynical, but is it because he loves accountants?"

Tauzin is the number 2 lifetime recipient among House members of money from the accounting industry, at $317,500.

In 2002 Congress finally passed a corporate reform bill (known as Sarbanes-Oxley for its two main sponsors, Senator Paul Sarbanes [D-MD] and Representative Michael Oxley [R-OH]). It created a new accounting oversight board, to strengthen auditing procedures. And it held CEOs and chief financial officers of companies directly responsible for the accuracy of financial statements, on pain of criminal fines. But it left several problems unsolved. In addition to failing to treat stock options as expenses, Congress also avoided voting on an amendment that would have allowed defrauded investors to sue lawyers and accountants along with corporate officers. One reason for the bill's problems: its lead sponsor in the House, Representative Oxley. Over his lifetime in office, he is the number 9 career recipient in the House of funds from the securities industry, at $507,000, and the number 5 recipient of accounting industry cash, at $250,000.

Unfortunately, not enough has changed since the Sarbanes-Oxley corporate reform act was signed into law. For example, the SEC has allowed auditors to do tax work for the companies they audit, a loophole that would have thrilled now-defunct Arthur Andersen. Corporate disclosure of financial information is improving at a "snail's pace," reports Reuters. Shareholders still have little say over executive compensation. Allies of the financial services industry are pushing legislation through Congress that would limit the power of state regulators to oversee brokerage firms—a bill that is widely seen as a slap at New York's crusading attorney general Eliot Spitzer. The high-tech sector is still on top in their battle to avoid having to count stock options as business expenses. Yes, a few wealthy high-profile Wall Street players, like Martha Stewart, have done the perp walk. And a couple of the bigger looters, like Jeffrey Skilling of Enron and Bernard Ebbers of World-Com, have been indicted for securities fraud and other crimes. Those examples may cause some on Wall Street to alter their behavior. Otherwise, it's all small change.

Ask Not What Enron Did for Them, Ask What They Did for Enron

Only two groups benefited from Enron's rise—top company executives and the politicians they contributed to. But while thousands of Enron employees and small investors lost billions, those same politicians continue to deny that all that money ever bought any special favors. Time to correct that record!

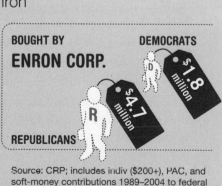

BOUGHT BY
ENRON CORP.
DEMOCRATS
$1.8 million
$4.7 million
REPUBLICANS

Source: CRP; includes indiv ($200+), PAC, and soft-money contributions 1989–2004 to federal candidates and parties

Between 1989 and 2002, Enron Corporation, its employees, and their families gave $6.5 million to federal parties and candidates, slightly more than half of that in soft money and the rest in hard money. Seventy-one percent went to Republicans, the rest to Democrats. At the peak of the company's influence in 2001, it had contributed to 71 serving Senators and 187 serving House members.

Enron got plenty for its cash:

- The ability to create a whole new unregulated business in energy derivatives which propelled the company to number 5 on the Fortune 500 list for 2001, when it claimed $139 billion in annual sales

- Extensive input in the writing of the Bush administration's proposed energy legislation (at least 17 planks of the Bush energy plan were supported by the company and/or would have benefited it financially)

- $7.2 billion in public financing from U.S. government and multilateral development banks to support Enron projects in 29 countries

- Handpicked choices for key government regulatory positions, including the chairman of the Federal Energy Regulatory Commission and the chairman of the Tennessee Valley Authority

- A delay in government intervention in California's energy crisis, including lengthy foot-dragging in the face of market manipulation by Enron and other energy companies

- Top-level calls from Bush and Clinton officials lobbying the governments of India and Mozambique on Enron's behalf

- An IRS that looked the other way while the company paid no taxes in four of the five years between 1996 and 2000 (by claiming tax savings from stock options and creating more than 800 subsidiaries in tax havens like the Cayman Islands)

Arthur Andersen, Enron's accounting firm, gave another $6.1 million, 62 percent to Republicans. This money worked to great effect when the time came to block SEC efforts to clamp down on the

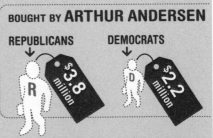

BOUGHT BY ARTHUR ANDERSEN

REPUBLICANS   **DEMOCRATS**

$3.8 million $2.2 million

Source: CRP; includes Indiv ($200+), PAC, and soft-money contributions 1989–2004 to federal candidates and parties

burgeoning and lucrative practice of selling consulting services to companies while auditing their books at the same time.

And yet, there are many prominent Americans who say Enron and Arthur Andersen's campaign contributions didn't buy them anything:

The Enron Hall of Shame

President George W. Bush: "You know, Enron had made contributions to a lot of people around Washington, D.C. And if they came to this administration looking for help, they didn't find any."

Vice President Dick Cheney: "The issue here isn't, with respect to Enron, isn't what advice they may have offered the energy task force. The issue, with respect to Enron, is the corporate collapse."

White House Spokesman Ari Fleischer (regarding calls Vice President Cheney made to Indian government officials on behalf of Enron): "I don't think you could say that they were influenced by the contributions that were given to the Bush campaign."

Commerce Secretary Donald Evans (former chair of the Bush-Cheney campaign): "All through the campaign, when I talked to people about making contributions, I said, 'For this contribution, you're going to get good government, you're going to get a president that has a great mind, a big heart and an extraordinary leader and this whole world can trust. And if you're looking for anything else, you got the wrong candidate.'"

Senator Mitch McConnell (R-KY): "This whole argument that influence is for sale is utter nonsense. What did Enron get? They got nothing, nothing whatsoever, except investigations, criminal prosecutions, subpoenas. They've gotten nothing but problems. Their contributions got them nothing."

Representative John Linder (R-GA): "It's silliness. If there's any evidence, bring it forth. And if there isn't, then don't keep implying that there might be."

Representative David Dreier (R-CA): "Those who will try to draw a correlation between the bankruptcy of Enron and the political process—obviously there is no correlation."

GOP national chair Marc Racicot: "I have not seen any evidence of any public official—whether Democrat or Republican—that reflects something that could be classified as wrongdoing. So even though there certainly have been campaign contributions received by people on both sides of the aisle, there does not appear to be any wrongdoing as a result of the participation of Enron in the political affairs of this nation."

DNC national chair Terry McAuliffe (after being asked about favors Clinton administration officials did on behalf of Enron, followed by the receipt of campaign contributions): "I'm not saying there's anything wrong with it. I haven't said there's anything wrong with what the Bush White House has done. . . . Our only point is we want disclosure."

***Weekly Standard* executive editor Fred Barnes:** "The bigger the contribution, the more favors the donor gets: That's the argument. Enron proves the opposite. . . . Their election donations bought them nothing."

TEST YOUR MONEY-IN-POLITICS IQ

What do all of the following people have in common?

a) **Former Christian Coalition head Ralph Reed**
b) **Marc Racicot, former chair of the Republican National Committee**
c) **Ed Gillespie, current chair of the Republican National Committee**
d) **Jack Quinn, former White House counsel to President Bill Clinton**
e) **U.S. Trade Representative Robert Zoellick**
f) **Republican pollster Frank Luntz**
g) **Former White House economic advisor Lawrence Lindsey**

Answer: They were all paid Enron lobbyists or consultants. And Gillespie and Quinn ran a lobbying practice together.

PART TWO

OUR HEALTH IS BEING ENDANGERED

"[Elections] have become a quasi-corporate process. . . . The big contributors [become] the major shareholders. The rest of the population is left just to vote, to affirm the management."

—Joe Scott, a political consultant to Senator Dianne Feinstein (D-CA), March 1994

THE INCREDIBLE SHRINKING HEALTH CARE DEBATE

The more money health care and insurance industry interests pour into campaigns, the smaller politicians' proposals to address the nation's health care crisis become. Coincidence? You be the judge. Meanwhile, one out of seven Americans lacks health insurance and the number keeps rising.

Dr. Arthur Kellerman is the chair of the department of emergency medicine at Emory University. A few years ago, he treated a middle-aged, working mother who had a massive stroke and then was brought to his emergency room in a coma. She died, "despite an all-out effort to save her," Dr. Kellerman later recalled. "In treating her, I learned she had stopped taking her blood pressure medicine two weeks before. Her blood pressure shot up, causing an artery in her brain to burst. Why had she stopped taking her medicine? Because she was poor and uninsured, and she had to choose between buying food for her kids or medicine for herself. Like most moms, she chose food, and paid for the decision with her life."

In the fall of 2003, Pete and Mary MacDowell of Chapel Hill, North Carolina, went shopping for individual health insurance. Pete had recently retired and his group insurance had expired. The couple applied for coverage from the Blue Cross Advantage Plan.

Though both are in their early 60s, neither has a serious health condition. Nor do they smoke, another red flag for insurance actuaries. Pete does have diabetes, but it's under control without medication, and his high blood pressure is also under control. "Nothing more than getting older," Pete told us in an e-mail. But when he heard back from Blue Cross, he could have had a heart attack. "The good news about this plan is that they would not reject you, just adjust the price according to the underwriting," he e-mailed some of his friends. "The quote: For a standard $500 deductible plan, no dental or glasses, for both of us: $4,189/mo. or $50,268/yr. For a stripped-down $5,000 deductible plan, $2,934/mo. or $35,208/yr."

With no irony or sarcasm, he added, "Time to riot."

Over 43 million Americans currently lack health insurance. Like Dr. Kellerman's patient, some 18,000 of them will die unnecessarily this year for that basic reason, according to a recent series of studies by the Institute of Medicine, an arm of the National Academy of Sciences.

In addition, one out of three Americans will probably experience a gap in coverage over the next four years, as they or other family members change jobs or lose coverage for other reasons. Contrary to conventional wisdom, lack of insurance is not solely tied to unemployment—in fact, 80 percent of the uninsured live in a home where at least one person works. Another trend that is driving up the number of uninsured—more companies are stripping health insurance out of their retirees' benefit packages.

While many of the uninsured do go to hospital emergency rooms to get essential treatment, they are not getting the same quality of medical care as people with insurance. Lack of insurance also leads to shorter lives, one major reason why the United States ranks 25th in male life expectancy and 19th in female life expectancy among 29 developed countries.

People who are uninsured get fewer preventive services—like regular checkups, mammograms, and prostate screenings. If they have a chronic condition like high blood pressure, asthma, or diabetes, they are less likely to obtain vital medications on a regular basis. In general, people without insurance are less likely to see a doctor, or even to have a regular doctor. And the lack of regular care can lead to more expensive care for preventable or treatable conditions. Ultimately, taxpayers, who pay almost $30 billion a year to cover unreimbursed medical expenses, absorb much of these costs.

Why is America doing so little about the crisis of the uninsured, especially when surveys show that more Americans worry about health care costs than about losing their job, paying their rent or mortgage, losing money in the stock market, or being a victim of a terrorist attack?

An even harder question: why are people with power in Washington proposing to do so much less about the uninsured than they did just a few years ago? This is true of both Republicans and Democrats, by the way.

In 1992 the first President Bush proposed to cover 85 percent of uninsured people by offering to spend $50 billion a year on tax credits that could amount to $5,100 per year per family. Nine years later, his son, George W. Bush, proposed a similar plan, only it was much stingier—covering just 14 percent of the uninsured at a cost of $9 billion a year.

Democrats have also scaled back their ambitions, which once—when Harry Truman ran for president—even included universal national health insurance. In 1993 President Bill Clinton and Hillary Rodham Clinton put forward a complicated plan that would have eventually provided public insurance to 95 percent of all Americans. Fast-forward to 1998–2000 and Democrats were focused on something they called the Patients' Bill of Rights, which would guarantee those with HMO coverage greater access to vital medical services and allow people

> * * * * *
>
> *"We are the only people in the world required by law to take large amounts of money from strangers and then act as if it has no effect on our behavior."*
>
> —*U. S. Representative Barney Frank (D-MA), quoted in "Coming to Terms: A Money in Politics Glossary," CRP*

to sue their insurer if it denied them needed care, but did nothing to expand coverage for the uninsured.

Why the incredible shrinking health care debate?

One big reason for this gap in legislative coverage can be summed up rather easily: uninsured Americans don't have a powerful lobby and they don't make campaign contributions. Making sure that everyone has health insurance means going after powerful moneyed interests that now dominate the health care business, and by extension, the political debate. As Representative Pete Stark (D-CA) said back in 1992, "The doctors don't like [national health insurance]. The hospitals don't like it. The drug companies don't like it, and the insurance companies don't like it."

The last time Washington tried to do anything serious about the health care crisis, in 1993–1994, groups representing these industries spent somewhere between $100 million and $300 million to lobby Congress and the public in defense of their interests, according to Haynes Johnson and David Broder, two veteran *Washington Post* reporters who wrote *The System,* a definitive reconstruction of the health care battles of the Clinton years. The insurance industry lobby was so strong that the Clintons rejected outright any discussion of a Canadian-style "single-payer" plan in favor of "managed competition," even though single-payer could cover everyone while saving hundreds of billions of dollars. The efforts by the insurance companies, doctors and hospitals, and the pharmaceutical industry—along with broader business lobbies like the National Federation of Independent Business and the Chamber of Commerce—to kill the Clinton bill "were almost indistinguishable from presidential campaign organizations in the scope of their fundraising, the scale of their field organizing, the sophistication of their advertising and public relations skills, and the speed of their electronic communications," Johnson and Broder write. Supporters of health care reform, by contrast, were divided and far less well funded.

Since then, health care reform has become a new "third rail of American politics"—an issue that politicians don't want to touch.

As Representative Patrick Kennedy (D-RI), who chaired the House Democrats' fund-raising arm in 1999–2000, admitted not long ago, the failure of Clinton-style health care reform taught Democrats that "to change the status quo here, we would have to overturn too many vested relationships."

One out of every seven dollars in the American economy is generated in the health care industry. So perhaps it's not surprising that the health sector has also been a generous contributor to political campaigns, furnishing over $478 million to federal candidates and parties since 1989. That includes money from health professionals, hospitals, nursing homes, medical suppliers, nutritional and dietary supplement makers, and pharmaceutical manufacturers. On top of that, the giant insurance sector provided $213.7 million.

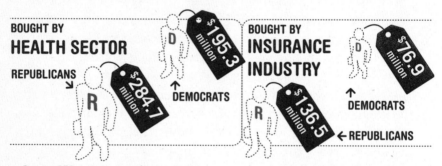

BOUGHT BY
HEALTH SECTOR
REPUBLICANS
R $284.7 million
D $195.3 million
↑ DEMOCRATS

BOUGHT BY
INSURANCE INDUSTRY
D $76.9 million
↑ DEMOCRATS
R $136.5 million
← REPUBLICANS

Source: CRP; includes indiv ($200+), PAC, and soft-money contributions 1989–2004 to federal candidates and parties

When politicians do approach health care, it's with far more incremental proposals, like a bill passed in 1996 that requires insurers to offer coverage to people when they lose or change jobs (without placing any limits on what they can charge), or efforts to get more children enrolled under Medicaid. Even the broadly popular notions that patients should be able to go to an emergency room without prior approval from their HMO or that patients should have the right to appeal restrictive care decisions made by their insurance company have foundered. These issues have been entangled in the fierce fight between trial lawyers and business groups over so-called tort reform.

The Association of Trial Lawyers of America is one of the richest Political Action Committees in the country—delivering over $22.9 million to candidates and parties since 1989, 85 percent to Democrats. Its leading adversary, the American Medical Association, isn't far behind, having given a tad over $20 million during that same period, 59 percent to Republicans. So far, these two sides have fought each other to a draw over the issue of arbitrarily capping medical malpractice awards.

All this money, and the lobbying that goes along with it, has had the effect of completely clogging the legislative arteries, blocking any consideration of fundamental solutions to the health care crisis. Each special interest group has subsidies it wants supported and privileges protected. But seen from the perspective of someone who is uninsured, Congress appears to be a private hospital that only treats paying patients, instead of a public institution accessible to all.

WHO WATCHES THE WATCHDOGS?

Since the early 1990s, pharmaceutical company money has flooded into Washington. Responding to pressure, the Food and Drug Administration has doubled the number of drugs it approves, in half the time it used to take to review them. The number of drugs pulled from the market for safety reasons has also soared, with drugs the FDA rushed to market at the behest of Big Pharma suspected as the cause of the deaths of over 1,000 patients. And is Congress investigating? Don't hold your breath.

On October 28, 1997, Scott Englebrick, a three-month-old baby, died after being given Propulsid, a new drug made by Janssen Pharmaceutica, a Johnson & Johnson Company subsidiary, to treat nighttime heartburn. A year earlier, the Food and Drug Administration had told the company that Propulsid was "not approvable" for children. However, in keeping with agency practice, that news was not made public. The drug had been okayed for general use in 1993, even though the medical officer examining it had found that it could cause heart rate and rhythm disorders. Eight children six years old or younger had died during tests, but the FDA official, who wasn't a cardiac specialist, agreed with the drug's maker that those deaths were due to other causes.

Two years after Propulsid went on the market, more negative reports coming into the FDA raised concerns. A senior medical officer met with Janssen executives to discuss the matter. They responded by saying the cases cited weren't "clean" enough to blame Propulsid. Instead of starting careful clinical studies to check for sure, the FDA and the company agreed to make changes in the drug's safety labeling, in the hopes that doctors would be cautious in how they prescribed it.

Meanwhile, lots of doctors were starting to give Propulsid to kids as a treatment for gastric reflux. Janssen says it didn't market the drug for children, but it did make generous grants to the North American Society for Pediatric Gastroenterolgy and Nutrition, whose literature advised doctors that Propulsid could be used safely and effectively in children. In August 1997 the doctor in charge of the FDA's gastrointestinal drugs division told Janssen that the agency was considering changing the drug's label to warn against giving it to babies, citing several deaths among children. However, the company didn't agree to those labeling changes until almost a year later. In the intervening months, Scott Englebrick died. The revised label noted that "several pediatric deaths" had occurred among children taking the drug but hedged as to whether Propulsid was at fault, saying, "Causality has not been established." Only in March 2000, after at least 302 deaths involving heart rhythm problems in which Propulsid was identified as the primary suspect—including 24 children under the age of six—was the drug pulled off the market.

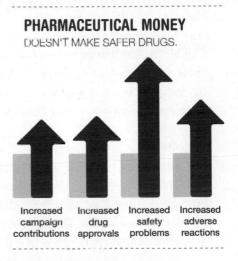

PHARMACEUTICAL MONEY
DOESN'T MAKE SAFER DRUGS.

Increased campaign contributions | Increased drug approvals | Increased safety problems | Increased adverse reactions

"If I had known that this drug caused cardiac arrhythmias, I would never have given it to him," said Tina Englebrick, Scott's mother. Her husband, Jeffrey, told David Hillman, the Pulitzer Prize–winning *Los Angeles Times* reporter who blew this story open, that he had no idea that the FDA had found Propulsid unfit for children a full year before they gave the drug to their infant son. "To me, that means they took my kid as a guinea pig to see if it would work."

In the seven years that Propulsid was on the U.S. market, it generated sales of $2.5 billion. During that same period from 1993 to 2000, Johnson & Johnson, the owner of Janssen, spent $1.2 million on campaign contributions to federal candidates, leadership PACs, and parties, part of the tens of millions invested by pharmaceutical companies seeking looser government regulation of their business.

Can money-in-politics kill you? A look at what has happened at the Food and Drug Administration (FDA) ever since the pharmaceutical industry started pushing to loosen the agency's process for reviewing the safety of new drugs suggests that the answer is yes.

In 1992 Congress passed the Prescription Drug User Fee Act, with significant prodding from the drug industry. The law called on the FDA to speed up its drug reviews, using a beefed-up staff paid for by charging drugmakers a hefty "user fee" for each new drug application they made. The FDA soon was reviewing twice as many drugs and ruling on them in half the time it used to take.

That wasn't enough for the pharmaceutical lobby, however. After Newt Gingrich's Republican rebels took over the House of Representatives in 1994, the FDA was vilified as a slow-moving bureaucracy in need of further reform. Gingrich called the agency "the leading job killer in America." Right-wing think tanks accused the FDA of murdering Americans by denying them access to new drugs.

In 1997 Congress passed, and President Clinton signed, the Food and Drug Administration Modernization Act, reducing the number of clinical trials needed for new drugs to just one, speeding up the approval process in other ways and allowing the promotion of FDA-okayed products for "off-label" uses—that is, for medical conditions unrelated to their original approved purpose.

The law, which was everything the drugmakers wanted, flew through Congress like a dose of salts, with few lawmakers voting against its final passage.

The vote on one amendment was indicative of the forces at work. Senator Richard Durbin (D-IL) proposed that private individuals and organizations reviewing new medical devices be subject to the same tough conflict-of-interest rules that govern FDA employees. (As is, the law allows medical device manufacturers to pay outside, for-profit reviewers to recommend approval of their products.) His amendment lost 59–40. On average, senators who voted against Durbin's proposal received almost $50,000 from the pharmaceutical industry over the prior six years, 45 percent more than senators who voted for the tougher rules.

THEY GAVE MONEY. THEY GOT VOTES. COINCIDENCE?

BIG PHARMA WANTED CONGRESS TO REJECT TOUGHER CONFLICT-OF-INTEREST RULES FOR REVIEWERS OF NEW MEDICAL DEVICES*

Senators who said:
SURE! got $49,800†

Senators who said:
NOPE! got $34,400†

*105th Congress, 1st Session, Senate vote #252, 40Y-59N. N=Industry position.
†CRP; includes indiv ($200+) and PAC contributions, average received, 1993–1998

Between 1970 and 1992 the FDA approved just nine drugs that were later recalled due to safety issues. But since Congress defanged the FDA, a record number of thirteen approved drugs had to be withdrawn from the market due to their lethal side effects. Not one of these dangerous drugs filled a medical need unmet by other drugs already on the market. Worse, the culture inside the FDA appears to have been drastically altered, from an agency devoted to protecting the public from unsafe drugs, to one devoted to working hand-in-glove with the pharmaceutical industry.

John Gueriguian, a veteran FDA officer who fought the approval of Rezulin, a diabetes drug that ultimately was pulled from the market after being linked to at least 391 deaths, says, "The people in charge don't say, 'Should we approve this drug?' They say, 'Hey, how can we get this drug approved?'"

Despite the rising hazards, Congress has given no indication of imposing tougher standards to protect public health. The reason, as noted earlier, can be traced to $108.4 million in individual, PAC, and soft-money contributions from the pharmaceutical sector since 1989, two-thirds to Republicans.

As Daniel Sigelman, a former Democratic congressional aide, has pointed out, compared to the years from the mid-1960s through the 1980s, when Congress often conducted investigations into dubious drugs and ferreted out weaknesses in the FDA's procedures, there has yet to be a congressional hearing examining of any of the thirteen dangerous drugs recalled since the 1997 law took effect. Representative Billy Tauzin (R-LA), until recently the chairman of the House Committee on Energy and Commerce, who

FIVE DEADLY DRUGS
THAT WERE APPROVED BY THE FDA

COMPANY	Johnson & Johnson	Warner-Lambert (Pfizer)*	American Home Products (Wyeth)*	Roche
DRUG	**Propulsid**	**Rezulin**	**Redux & Duract**	**Posicor**
U.S. SALES (MILLIONS)	**$2,500**	**$2,100**	**$345**	**$25.6**
CAMPAIGN CONTRIBUTIONS 1993–2000†	$1,212,400	$2,987,400	$1,805,800	$1,504,600
DEATHS (1993–2000)	**302**	**391**	**191**	**100**

Source: CRP, FDA, *Los Angeles Times* *Pfizer bought Warner-Lambert in 2000; American Home Products changed its name to Wyeth in 2002. †Includes indiv ($200+), PAC, and soft-money contributions to federal candidates, leadership PACs, and parties

oversees the industry, ranks thirteenth in the House in his total receipts from pharmaceutical company campaign givers, with over $272,000. His colleague Representative James Greenwood (R-PA), who runs the committee's investigative panel, is the number 20 recipient of funds from the industry, with over $179,000.

Representative Sherrod Brown, a ranking Democrat on Tauzin's committee, has tried to raise questions about the FDA's cozy relationship with the pharmaceutical industry, with little success. He complains, "This committee and this Congress jump when the drug industry says jump. . . . When the drug industry wants us to move quickly to ensure that the FDA doesn't hold up their products from getting to the market, we move with lightning speed to do their bidding."

More than half of the new drug reviewers at the FDA said that the six months allotted for reviewing priority drug applications (for breakthrough drugs or those designed to treat unusual conditions) was inadequate, according to a recent survey by the inspector general of the U.S. Department of Health and Human Services. One in five said they felt pressure to recommend drugs despite reservations about a drug's safety or effectiveness. The agency's current chief counsel, Daniel Troy, appointed by President Bush, was previously a lawyer for the tobacco and pharmaceutical industries who once clerked for conservative judge Robert Bork. Under his supervision, the number of enforcement

* * * * *

"Sophisticated political donors . . . are not in the business of dispensing their money purely on ideological or charitable grounds. Rather, these political donors typically are trying to wisely invest their resources to maximize political return."

—*Wright H. Andrews, past president of the American League of Lobbyists, whose firm earned $6 million between 1997 and 2000 alone lobbying for such savvy investors as the American Bankers Association, British Airways, Charter One Bank, the Coalition to Amend the Financial Privacy Information Act, Derivatives Net Inc., the Dime Savings Bank of NY, Federated Department Stores, and Peoples Bank*

letters sent by the agency to stop misleading advertising by drug companies has dropped by two-thirds, according to *U.S. News* and *World Report*. Troy has held at least fifty private meetings with drug makers since coming to the FDA; his office told the magazine there are "no minutes, no memos, no nothing," on what was discussed.

TEST YOUR MONEY-IN-POLITICS IQ

Which of the following statements is true?

a. **The Food and Drug Administration has the power to order the recall of deadly drugs.**
b. **Government researchers overseeing the testing of prescription drugs are not allowed to receive payments from the makers of those drugs.**
c. **The FDA independently tests the safety and effectiveness of new drugs.**
d. **Pharmaceutical manufacturers are legally prohibited from advertising drugs for uses for which they have not been approved by the FDA.**
e. **No congressional committee has investigated why the FDA approved 13 dangerous prescription drugs that have since been withdrawn from the market by their manufacturers.**

Answer: e. Even after more than a thousand patients died and thousands were injured, there have been no congressional hearings into whether the FDA has sped up the approval process to the detriment of public safety.

Pumped Up

At the end of December 2003, the Food and Drug Administration announced that it was banning ephedra, a nutritional supplement linked to thousands of health complaints and dozens of deaths. This is good news for American consumers, especially young people who were influenced by advertising touting ephedra's value as a diet pill and energy booster. But a cautionary tale about the power of money in politics remains. Even though ephedra is being removed from the market, nutritional supplement makers still don't have to prove the safety or efficacy of their products thanks to a 1994 law backed by the industry.

Ten things you should know about the ephedra story:

1. Ephedra is an herb (known in China as ma huang), the botanical kin to the chemical compound ephedrine, a component of methamphetamine. Like synthetic amphetamines, it elevates heart rate and blood pressure.

2. The FDA banned the use of ephedrine in over-the-counter drugs in 1983. But as a naturally occurring herb, ephedra comes under the 1994 Dietary Supplements Health and Education Act, which regulates diet supplements as foods, not drugs. This means that companies do not have to prove supplements are safe or effective before selling them. Instead, the FDA has to prove a supplement is unsafe before it can restrict its use. Supplement makers are not required to alert the FDA when they receive health complaints.

3. Ephedra was a huge hit with dieters and athletes, including many young people. Sales hit $1.3 billion in 2002, according to *Nutrition Business Journal*.

4. In 1997 reports of deaths, heart attacks, strokes, and seizures among ephedra users prompted the FDA to propose limits on its use. State health authorities and legislators in Texas and California began to take similar steps. This set off a wave of influence buying by Metabolife, the biggest marketer of ephedra, and other companies in the $19 billion nutritional supplement industry.

5. Senator Orrin Hatch (R-UT) was the principal author of the 1994 law, along with Senator Tom Harkin (D-IA). They both wrote letters to the FDA questioning its handling of ephedra. So did Representative Brian Bilbray (R-CA). Hatch and Harkin are the Senate's number 1 and number 2 lifetime recipients of campaign cash from the nutritional and dietary supplements sector, at $156,950 and $125,580, respectively. Hatch's son Scott has also been retained as a lobbyist by an industry trade association. Bilbray tops the House list of all-time recipients at $54,750. (Metabolife is based in his district.) Overall, the industry gave $5.5 million to federal candidates and parties from 1989 to the present, nearly $2 million of which came from Metabolife between 1997 and 2002, when the FDA was most actively investigating ephedra. Talk about getting pumped up! The agency backed down during that period.

6. In Texas in 1999, Metabolife's lobbyists blocked a move by health authorities to require a prescription for ephedra. Then-governor George

W. Bush received at least $40,000 in contributions from Metabolife executives and lobbyists and then intervened in the regulatory process to the company's benefit. (Bush '04 Ranger and '00 Pioneer Tom Loeffler was a Metabolife lobbyist.) A year later in California in 2000, then-governor Gray Davis took $175,000 in contributions from Metabolife around the same time that the state assembly was moving to require warning labels on products containing ephedra. Davis vetoed the bill.

7.   In 2001 Public Citizen asked the FDA to ban ephedra, citing reports of 81 deaths along with other serious medical conditions caused by its use, and noting that Canadian health authorities had just banned the substance. U.S. military authorities halted sales of ephedra products at commissaries that year, but the FDA still did not take action.

8.   In October 2002 Senator Richard Durbin (D-IL), a longtime critic of the supplement industry as well as the pharmaceutical industry, held a hearing on the dangers of ephedra. Beforehand, "Colleagues of mine in the Senate from both parties came to me and said, 'You can't do this. This is not in your jurisdiction. You ought to stay away from it,'" he later told National Public Radio. "Then they'd pull me over to the side and say quietly, 'This industry is a big supporter. They help us. A lot of their people are big Democrats and, you know, you ought to think twice about this.' And I thought to myself, 'This is unbelievable.'"

9.   In July 2002 FDA chief counsel Daniel Troy "stalled efforts to investigate complaints about ephedra," *U.S. News and World Report* later revealed. The Justice Department had offered to help the agency obtain Metabolife documents detailing more than 13,000 consumer complaints the company had received about the drug, but Troy balked.

10. Only after the ephedra-linked death of Baltimore Orioles pitcher Steve Bechler in February 2003 did Congress hold hearings on ephedra's dangers. By the time the FDA finally banned it, most companies had already stopped selling the product. The action came almost 10 years after medical authorities spotted problems with the substance. At least 164 deaths have been connected to its use.

Postscript: Though President Bush called for tougher controls on steroid abuse in his January 2004 State of the Union address, he made no mention of ephedra, which has been much more widely used. So far, there are no signs that Congress will revisit the 1994 law that allows makers of nutritional supplements to sell their products without proving their safety or effectiveness. With ephedra banned, retailers are turning to replacements like bitter orange, which is derived from citrus fruits. The FDA recently disclosed that bitter orange, which has ephedra-like effects though it is based on a different chemical, has been associated with seven deaths. Acting FDA Commissioner Lester Crawford says it is "too soon to say" whether it should be banned from the market. The agency's supplement division employs about 60 people, about one-fiftieth the number who oversee pharmaceutical drugs. In April 2004, Consumers Union, which says the FDA is badly "understaffed and underfunded," released a "dirty dozen" list of dangerous supplements like bitter orange that are widely available and dangerous to users' health.

WHEN IS A DRUG NOT A DRUG?

It's addictive, it's hazardous to your health, its makers hide what they put in it, and young people are especially prone to getting hooked on it. But the Food and Drug Administration can't regulate it. That's because it's tobacco.

The answer to the rhetorical question posed by the title of this chapter is: A drug isn't a drug when the industry that makes it has contributed over $51.9 million to federal candidates and party committees since 1989. That's how much green stuff the tobacco industry has puffed into the air around Congress and the White House, according to the Center for Responsive Politics.

There are lots of reasons why tobacco ought to fall under the authority of the FDA. Tobacco products are addictive; they cause cancer and other life-shortening illnesses; consumers deserve full information on all the additives they contain (like formaldehyde, arsenic, and ammonia); their packaging carries limited health warnings; they are often marketed to young people; long-burning cigarettes are prone to start fires. All of these concerns could be addressed by FDA oversight.

Yet even after the tobacco companies' $246 billion settle-

BOUGHT BY **TOBACCO INDUSTRY** REPUBLICANS — DEMOCRATS
R $39 million
D $13 million

Source: CRP; includes indiv ($200+), PAC, and soft-money contributions 1989–2004 to federal candidates and parties

ment deal in 1999 with 46 states that had sued to recover tobacco-related health costs, big money from Big Tobacco has stymied all efforts in Congress to bring tobacco under FDA jurisdiction. According to the Campaign for Tobacco-Free Kids, more than 4 million children have become daily smokers in the meantime. The tobacco settlement called for the companies to restrict their marketing efforts and to contribute $1.5 billion to a public education effort to reduce tobacco use. However, today spending on tobacco marketing outpaces state tobacco control spending by about 50–1.

* * * * *

"Some lobbyists continue to support the present campaign finance system because their own abilities to influence decisions, and their economic livelihoods, are far more dependent on using political contributions and expenditures than on the merits of their causes."

—Wright H. Andrews Jr., past president of the American League of Lobbyists, declaration for McConnell v. FEC

In 2001–2002, more than half the members of the U.S. House were happy to accept contributions from tobacco interests, averaging just over $8,100 each. Forty-nine senators also took tobacco cash that election cycle, at a clip of $11,225 each. And then there's President Bush, who inhaled over $91,000 from tobacco in his 2000 campaign, plus another $100,000 for his first inaugural. For his reelection, his take from tobacco was running at an even faster pace, having totaled $133,150 as reported by January 31, 2004.

But if you only look at tobacco giving to individual politicians, you miss the forest for the trees. Since 1999, the bulk of tobacco money has flowed directly to the Republican party's main fund-raising arms—the Republican National Committee (RNC), the National Republican Senatorial Committee (NRSC), which supports Senate candidates, and the National Republican Congressional Committee (NRCC), which supports House candidates.

One company, Philip Morris, the largest tobacco company in the world, has provided a giant share of this cash. It has consistently ranked in or near the top five individual companies providing money to Republican Party fund-raising committees. According to the Center for Responsive Politics, the company ranks number 10 among its Top 100 All-Time Individual Donors, giving $20.3 million since 1989, 75 percent to Republicans.

Even though the bulk of the money Big Tobacco gave to the national Republican Party was in the form of soft money, which the national party committees can no longer raise under the 2002 Bipartisan Campaign Reform Act, the industry's investment is still paying dividends.

In the 2001–2002 election cycle, Congress debated two different approaches to granting the FDA authority over tobacco. One bill, backed by the public health community, would give the FDA meaningful and effective power to regulate tobacco. The other bill, sponsored by Senate Majority Leader Bill Frist (R-TN) and Representative Tom Davis (R-VA), was opposed by every major public health organization. They complained that it included loopholes that would make it harder for the FDA to restrict tobacco ads impacting children or to require changes in tobacco products to reduce the harm they cause. While neither Frist nor Davis personally were recipients of significant sums from Big Tobacco, it is no coincidence, health advocates say, that they were the respective chairs of the NRSC/NRCC during the years that these two Republican party fund-raising committees took in millions from the industry.

BIG TOBACCO & REPUBLICANS
KEEPING THE FDA AT BAY

4.2 MILLION

2.4 MILLION

2.7 MILLION

2001–2002

1999–2000

RNC   NRSC   NRCC

*Source: CRP; includes indiv ($200+), soft-money, and PAC contributions

Neither bill passed. In 2003 the two sides again clashed in Congress. This time, public health groups and congressmen from non-tobacco-growing states tried to forge an alliance with struggling tobacco farmers—linking support for FDA tobacco regulation to a bill calling for the tobacco companies to put up $15 billion to buy out the farmers' tobacco-growing quotas (a holdover from the Depression years, when the quotas propped up prices). But hopes for a bill died after Senator Edward Kennedy (D-MA) and then representative Ernie Fletcher (R-KY) hit an impasse over the bill's details. Tobacco lobbyists insisted on weakening the FDA's proposed authority to the point of stating that the agency couldn't "directly or indirectly" ban any tobacco product, under the proposed bill language. And so the public health community withdrew its support for a compromise. Representative Fletcher took almost $90,000 from the tobacco industry during his five years in Congress, putting him at number 24 lifetime among all recipients of tobacco money in the House. (He was elected governor of Kentucky in 2003.) Senator Kennedy has taken $9,250.

The issue will no doubt come up again. But in the meantime, hundreds of thousands more children will take up smoking, lured by ads that still target them and untouched by underfunded state programs to help them make better choices.

TEST YOUR MONEY-IN-POLITICS IQ

Which of the following products is not regulated by the Food and Drug Administration?

a. **Frozen nonmeat pizza**
b. **Condoms**
c. **Pacemakers**
d. **Cell phones**
e. **Cigarettes**

Answer: e.

NOT ANYBODY'S IDEA OF A "HAPPY MEAL"

A toothless U.S. Department of Agriculture puts consumers at risk of biting into infected meat, thanks to the influence of the meat industry, which has fattened up Washington politicians with millions of dollars in campaign money.

"Visible fecal material on the neck, armpit, underneath the fore-shanks, and underneath the brisket area of two carcass sides."

Sounds delicious, huh? Like what you'd like to sit down to for dinner tonight? The unfortunate fact is, you may have already eaten meat like this, risking your health in the process—and thanks to the influence of campaign contributions from meat and poultry processors, the government won't do much about it.

The idea of feces on carcasses that will eventually become somebody's hamburger dinner isn't just something to feel grossed out about. It's a warning sign for anybody who knows anything about a certain strain of the bacterium *E. coli*. The bacterium is commonly found in the intestines of healthy humans and animals. But this strain produces a powerful toxin. People who eat it may be stricken with bloody diarrhea, occasionally kidney failure, and even death. Carcasses contaminated with feces may harbor this nasty strain of *E. coli*, which causes 73,000 cases of infection and 61 deaths in the United States each year, according to the Centers for Disease Control (CDC).

But the U.S. Department of Agriculture (USDA) can't shut a plant down when *E. coli* infection is suspected. The description above is from real life—a citation by the U.S. Department of Agriculture (USDA) presented to Nebraska Beef, Ltd., an Omaha-based meat-processing plant, reported by the *New York Times*. After two years' worth of similar infractions, in early 2003, the USDA, suspecting *E. coli* infection, attempted to shut down Nebraska Beef, to prevent food safety disasters in the making. But Nebraska Beef objected, pushed its case in court, and a few weeks later, the USDA backed off and settled out of court.

Why? The USDA lacks the explicit legal authority to shut down plants for unsanitary conditions. "The settlement suggests the Agriculture Department has no authority to close any plant based on public health considerations," said Carol Tucker Foreman, director of the Consumer Federation of America's Food Policy Institute.

"Now every plant in the nation knows that, for practical purposes, USDA can't shut them down for food safety violations."

Indeed, the case of Nebraska Beef is not an exception, it's the rule. The USDA has been losing in court when it has attempted to shut down processing plants that violate sanitary standards. In December 2001 the Fifth Circuit Court of Appeals affirmed that the USDA could not shut down the Dallas-based Supreme Beef Processors Inc., even though it had failed a test for salmonella infestation, another bacterium. Twice in recent years, Senator Tom Harkin (D-IA) has attempted to give the USDA explicit authority to shut down dirty meat plants. Both times the Senate rejected his amendments, the first time, in 2000, on a vote of 48 to 49, the second, in 2001, on a vote of 50 to 45. In both cases, senators who voted against Harkin's amendment received substantial campaign contributions from the food and meat-processing industries, while those who supported giving USDA authority received far less.

What's even worse, USDA inspectors are so toothless that they do not have the power to assess civil fines for unsanitary conditions in meatpacking plants. Here again, the meat processors have blocked change. In 1998 Representative Nita Lowey (D-NY), offered an

THEY GAVE MONEY. THEY GOT VOTES. COINCIDENCE?

THE MEAT-PROCESSING INDUSTRY WANTED CONGRESS TO KEEP THE USDA FROM SHUTTING DOWN DIRTY MEAT PLANTS.*

Senators who said:

SURE! got **$87,200**[†]

Senators who said:

NOPE! got **$43,100**[†]

*106th Congress, 2nd session, Vote # 221, 48Y–49N, N=industry position
[†]CRP, includes indiv ($200+) and PAC contributions, average received, 1995–2000

amendment that would have given the USDA power to assess fines. This measure, however, never even made it to the full House floor for a debate. Instead, the House Appropriations Committee rejected it by a vote of 25 to 19. On average, the 25 members who voted against Lowey's motion received six times as much in campaign contributions from the meat and poultry industry (in that election cycle) as the 19 who voted for it. The leading opponents of Lowey's proposal, Representatives Jack Kingston (R-GA) and Tom Latham (R-IA), were at the time respectively the number 1 and number 4 recipients of meat and poultry dollars on the Appropriations Committee.

Congress is not the only culprit. The USDA, under President George W. Bush, delayed and then weakened USDA regulations that would require companies to test their products for listeria monocytogenes, another deadly pathogen, which kills 20 percent of the people who develop severe infections.

In October 2002 Wampler Foods agreed to recall 27.4 million pounds of turkey and chicken, the largest meat recall in USDA's history because samples were contaminated with listeria monocytogenes.

Nearly two million pounds of the turkey meat linked with listeria found its way into schools, where cafeterias continued to serve it for five days before federal officials told school administrators that the meat was included in the recall.

By the time the outbreak had run its course, more than 120 people had become sick with listeriosis and 13 died after contracting the disease—illnesses and deaths that would have been preventable if the Bush administration had not postponed the regulation, according to consumer groups.

The National Food Processors Association, the food industry lobby, took credit for shaping a directive made by Agriculture Secretary Ann Veneman in the wake of the outbreak, issued in December 2002. Plans were dropped from an earlier version to fine companies where listeria was discovered, and testing was more limited.

In a November 11, 2002, members-only newsletter obtained by *Time* magazine, the NFPA gloated over its victory, saying that "a number of key (USDA) personnel have bought into much of the industry proposal." The newsletter added that the tougher federal rules were averted as a result of "industry efforts made at the White House level." The NFPA refused to comment. The White House denied the association had any role in the final rules. USDA undersecretary Elsa Murano acknowledged to *Time* that she had consulted both the White House and industry before the final directive was issued but insisted it was "fine-tuned" solely to advance public health.

Not long after watering down the inspection directive, the NFPA sponsored a food safety summit in March 2003. Participating in the summit were top leaders from the processing, restaurant, and retail food industry, representatives from Capitol Hill, key regulatory officials, and the White House. One of the main topics of discussion at the event was titled "Listeria's Hot Again: Why You Should Be Testing and How to Validate Your Testing Program." In June 2003 the USDA issued final regulations on listeria that were roundly criticized by consumer groups for being too weak.

* * * * *

"The general public does not even begin to understand the degree to which moneyed private interests are able to influence public policy through their campaign contributions."

—**Robert Rozen, lobbyist with Washington Council Ernst & Young,** *declaration for* McConnell v. FEC

With a toothless government watching over the food supply, the old adage rings true: watch what you eat.

Test Your Money-in-Politics IQ

Which of the following does the U.S. Department of Agriculture have the authority to do?

a. **Stop the unlicensed sale of dogs and cats**
b. **Punish circuses for mistreating elephants**
c. **Penalize watermelon salesmen for failing to keep appropriate records**
d. **Assess civil fines for unsanitary conditions in meatpacking plants**

Answer: a, b, and c. The USDA has authority to do all of the above except d.

Mad about Mad Cows

People who contract variant Creutzfeldt-Jakob disease after eating meat infected by mad cow disease, aka bovine spongiform encephalopathy (BSE), don't necessarily know it right away. They may have trouble sleeping, get depressed, or have trouble remembering things. But any number of things can cause these problems. As the disease advances, what started as memory loss progresses rapidly into dementia. By the final stages, a patient would most likely lapse into a coma before dying. The disease is incurable.

With more than 183,000 cases of BSE diagnosed in animals in the United Kingdom alone since the late 1980s, nearly 140 people dead, and the emergence of the disease recently in our neighbor to the north, Canada, you would think the United States government would have taken all measures necessary to protect the food supply. Yet it wasn't until a week after the U.S. Department of Agriculture (USDA) announced the first diagnosis of a cow with BSE in Washington State in late December 2003 that the agency finally banned the use of "downer" cattle, that is, cows that are not ambulatory, along with body parts suspected of harboring the disease, including the skull, brain, eyes, and spinal cord. By then, the American beef industry had already suffered a calamitous crash in prices and the disappearance of its multibillion-dollar export market.

What explains the governmental inertia on mad cow disease? At least part of the answer is the well-organized, well-funded lobby in Washington of cattlemen and food processors, which has successfully blocked stronger safety rules, rewarding politicians with nearly $92 million in campaign contributions since 1989.

What's worse, even now the agency is still not doing all it could. The main way cattle become infected with BSE is by eating other infected animals. While the United States banned the use of cattle in feed for other ruminants—cows, goats, and sheep—back in 1997, there is no such requirement for feed destined for chickens and other animals, which don't develop the dis-

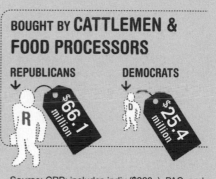

BOUGHT BY CATTLEMEN & FOOD PROCESSORS

REPUBLICANS   DEMOCRATS

R $66.1 million   D $25.4 million

Source: CRP; includes indiv ($200+), PAC, and soft-money contributions 1989–2004 to federal candidates and parties

ease themselves. In late January 2004 the government announced a new ban on feeding blood or poultry litter to cows, but it remains legal to feed rendered beef to pigs and poultry, and then to feed these animals to cows. Those new rules don't go far enough, according to an international panel of experts that Agriculture Secretary Ann Veneman appointed to evaluate the government's response to the crisis. "If we don't accept and implement measures, strong measures, we have this amplification cycle going on, and then we have a big problem," said Ulrich Kihm, a Swiss veterinarian, who was hired by the panel to help with the analysis.

Safety experts also think that the United States should be testing more cows for the disease. The same international panel recommended that the United States should do as other countries do. In France, half of the six million cows slaughtered annually are tested, and in Japan, all cows slaughtered are tested. In contrast, the U.S. Agriculture Department plans to test 40,000 cows out of some 36 million slaughtered. Indeed, in April 2004 the Agriculture Department even forbade one small Kansas-based company, Creekstone Farms Premium Beef, from testing *all* the cattle it slaughters, saying there was "no scientific justification" for it. (The company wanted to do the testing because without it, a major customer, Japan, had stopped buying its products.) Experts say that simply testing sick "downer" cows isn't enough, since the disease can set in before a cow shows any symptoms. Dave Louthan, the Washington State slaughterhouse worker who killed the cow that tested positive for the disease last December, has stated that the cow was not a "downer." Dr. Michael C. Hansen, a food safety expert with Consumers Union, told the *New York Times* that more testing would inevitably lead to finding more mad cow cases. "That was the pattern in Europe," he said. "Blanket denials, then you find one, then once you go to widespread testing, you find more and more and more."

This record of complacency is all the more astonishing given all the warnings that have been raised about the risks of mad cow disease. For years consumer groups have been urging the USDA and the Food and Drug Administration (FDA) to strengthen laws protecting the public from BSE. Back in 1997, writers Sheldon Rampton and John Stauber published *Mad Cow USA: Could the Nightmare Happen Here?* Yes, it could, they presciently concluded. But while their book received favorable reviews from publications such as the *Journal of the American Medical Association* and *New Scientist,* it was all but ignored by the mainstream media, quite possibly because newspaper publishers and TV broadcasters feared losing millions in lucrative advertising from beef producers.

The number one recipient of campaign dollars from the food-processing and livestock industries so far in the 2004 election, as well as in the 2000 elections, is President George W. Bush, with a grand total of nearly $2.5 million. (In the 1996 elections, back when mad cow was emerging as a threat, Bill Clinton received $84,200 from these industries.)

According to the *New York Times,* at a White House Christmas party, Bush told the president of the National Cattlemen's Beef Association, "I love those cattlemen!"

Since the president took office, he has appointed at least a dozen officials to the Department of Agriculture who have either worked for agriculture interests or lobbied for them, including Dr. Chuck Lambert, formerly the chief economist for the National Cattlemen's Beef Association, now deputy undersecretary for marketing and regulatory programs. Among the Bush-Cheney campaign's mega-fund-raisers called Rangers (those who raise at least $200,000) and Pioneers (those who raise at least $100,000) are at least three cattlemen: Tobin Armstrong, owner of Armstrong Ranch; Tom Bivens, the owner of Corsino Cattle Company; and Fausto Yturria Jr., owner of Yturria Ranch.

In February 2004 federal officials gave up on finding all of the cows that had entered the United States from Canada along with the infected Holstein in Washington State. Only one-third of the 80 animals were located, including 11 cows that were born around the same time as the infected cow and therefore were considered to be at higher risk for the disease, since they likely ate the same feed. "The paper trail has gotten cold; we have not been able to trace those animals," W. Ron DeHaven, chief veterinary officer at the Department of Agriculture told the *Washington Post*. "Some of them very likely have gone to slaughter." Back in December a USDA official had said, "We feel confident that we are going to be able to determine the whereabouts of most, if not all, of these animals within the next several days."

DARE YOUR KID EAT A PEACH?

Studies show that kids are particularly vulnerable to harm from exposure to pesticides. The law says that the Environmental Protection Agency is supposed to protect kids accordingly when regulating how much of a particular pesticide is allowed on food. Why isn't the government doing the job right? Could it be because of the millions of dollars contributed by the pesticide industry?

If you see a kid eating a juicy, fresh peach, you might think approvingly, "Now there's one kid who isn't eating junk." Peaches are wholesome. Peaches are nutritious. Peaches pack a punch of vitamin A, vitamin C, riboflavin, and beta carotene, and furthermore, they are fat-, sodium-, and cholesterol-free, all good stuff. In a nation beset with an epidemic of childhood obesity, a kid who eats peaches is, well, peachy.

Except there is one problem. Peaches are not pesticide free. Far from it, in fact. Peaches may contain residues of such tasty chemicals as chlorothalonil, a fungicide classified by the Environmental Protection Agency (EPA) as a likely carcinogen, and methomyl, a neurotoxin. Indeed a typical peach may well contain residues of three or more pesticides. And this isn't the only healthy produce that packs a hidden danger. Strawberries, pears, grapes, green beans, tomatoes, peas, spinach, peppers, melons, lettuce, squashes, and juice all are likely to contain pesticide residues.

Children are more vulnerable to harmful effects from pesticides than adults, concluded a 1993 study by the National Academy of Sciences. Their small bodies absorb proportionately more of the chemicals than adults do when they eat food that has been sprayed with chemicals, or when they are exposed to buildings or lawns where pesticides have been sprayed. Exposure to pesticides during pregnancy can heighten a child's risk of developing leukemia and other cancers, as well as increase miscarriage rates and birth defects. Children exposed to pesticides used commonly in grape vineyards developed cognitive problems such as reduced attention spans, impaired memory, and poor hand-eye coordination, according to research sponsored by the French Ministry of Environment. Evidence is also growing that exposure to pesticides early in life may play an important role in whether a person develops Parkinson's disease four or five decades later.

> * * * * *
>
> "While many members will deny it, the fact is they do not want to cross certain constituencies because it represents too much of the money they need."
>
> —Former Representative Tim Penny (D-MN), quoted in Speaking Freely 1st edition, CRP

Concern that environmental laws were not adequately protecting children from pesticide exposure inspired Congress in 1996 to unanimously approve the Food Quality Protection Act. The new law required the U.S. Environmental Protection Agency to consider the health of children and infants when determining how much pesticide residue should be allowed on fruits, vegetables, and other foods. Because of children's particular vulnerability to the chemicals, the EPA was instructed to err on the side of caution by using a tenfold margin of safety when setting limits. The agency was permitted to use a weaker standard if, and only if, it could prove, using reliable data, that the level of pesticide residue would be safe for infants and children.

In addition, the agency was to take into account, when judging safe levels of the chemicals, all the many ways children might be exposed to pesticides—whether through food, water, or in their own houses. Finally, the law required that the EPA consider together pesticides that share a common method of toxicity, so that safety standards would take into account the cumulative effect of chemicals of a particular type that a child might be exposed to, rather than analyzing them one by one.

The new law translated into a lot of work for the agency. There are some 500 pesticide chemicals registered for use on crops destined for your kitchen table, all of which needed to be reviewed. The agency would need to set new standards for the 9,600 pesticide "tolerances"—EPA's term for the exact limit of pesticide residue allowed on each type of food—apples, peaches, grapes, and so forth.

First on the EPA's review list was a class of chemicals known as organophosphates. These chemicals, along with the carbamates, kill insects by attacking their nervous systems, inhibiting enzymes that help transmit nerve signals. They are popular, low-cost pesticides used widely on crops, including fruits and vegetables, staples in children's diets.

At the time, the Environmental Working Group, a nonprofit environmental research organization, estimated that, every day, 1 out of 20 children ages five and under was eating an unsafe dose of organophosphate pesticides, contained in such foods as apple juice, pears, peaches, grapes, and corn chips.

Early in 1998 rumors were flying that the EPA might ban all organophosphates as part of its implementation of the Food Quality Protection Act. The pesticide industry and the agriculture interests that use these chemicals on crops quickly mobilized, seeking help from their friends in Congress.

Leading the counterattack was Representative Charlie Stenholm (D-TX), recipient of more than a quarter of a million dollars in campaign contributions from pesticide manufacturers and related concerns between 1991 and 1998. In the 1998 election cycle alone, he ranked first among his House colleagues for contributions from pesticide interests, receiving $43,900, almost three times as much as any other House member.

In February 1998 Stenholm and fellow House Agriculture Committee member Marion Berry (D-AR), then number 5 in the House in pesticide-related contributions, met with Vice President Al Gore and urged delay. They reportedly warned Gore—who was then gearing up to run for president—of potential trouble in key electoral states,

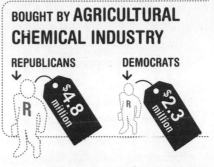

BOUGHT BY AGRICULTURAL CHEMICAL INDUSTRY

REPUBLICANS   DEMOCRATS

$4.8 million $2.3 million

Source: CRP; includes indiv ($200+), PAC, and soft-money contributions 1989–2004 to federal candidates and parties

such as Iowa, Texas, Florida, and California, if the EPA went ahead.

Two months later, Gore issued a memorandum essentially ordering the EPA to slow down as it evaluated organophosphates. His memo directed the agency to work with the Agriculture Department (traditionally more sympathetic to the industry's views), pay close attention to economic concerns, and ensure that the industry had a say in the proceedings. This led to the creation of a new 50-member committee, the Tolerance Reassessment Advisory Committee, to advise the EPA as it implemented the Food Quality Protection Act. Members include such pesticide manufacturers—and Stenholm donors—as Monsanto and the American Crop Protection Association, the trade association for the pesticide industry, along with some consumer and environmental representatives. Overall, the agricultural chemical industry has contributed $7.1 million to federal campaigns since 1989.

But the consumer and environmental representatives didn't last long on the EPA advisory committee. In April 1999, frustrated by the EPA's foot-dragging, the World Wildlife Fund, the Natural Resources Defense Council, the Pesticide Education Center, Consumers Union, the Farmworker Justice Fund, the National Campaign for Pesticide Reform, and the Farmworker Support Committee all announced their resignations. The Environmental Working Group had already walked out the previous October, complaining that the committee had "produced absolutely nothing that remotely resembles a plan or schedule to reduce pesticide risks."

Indeed, it was not until after the EPA was sued, first by the pesticide industry and farm groups, then by environmental groups (albeit for very different reasons), all complaining about implementation of the Food Quality Protection Act, that the EPA did finally develop a plan and a schedule. In 2001 the agency agreed to meet specific timetables to reassess pesticides, including a group of 11 organophosphate pesticides considered to be the most dangerous. However, when the agency claimed success in meeting its goals the following year, NRDC senior attorney Erik Olson stated,

"EPA is using Enron-like accounting to claim that it has met the mandate of the law. . . . EPA's delay only benefits the chemical industry at the expense of our children's health."

In September 2003 the attorneys general of Connecticut, Massachusetts, New Jersey, and New York sued the agency again, charging that the EPA had neglected to err on the side of caution, as required, when setting the safety factor meant to protect kids when reevaluating certain pesticides used on food. For example, the attorneys general charged that the agency had reduced the tenfold safety factor for chlorothalonil, despite the fact it lacked data on the cumulative risk of the pesticide, its neurotoxity, and its effect on the endocrine system.

"Sadly, the Environmental Protection Agency has failed to meet congressional requirements to protect children from the risks of consuming food with unhealthy pesticide residues," said New York Attorney General Eliot Spitzer, lead plaintiff in the case. NRDC and several other environmental groups filed a complementary lawsuit.

With pesticide policy tied down in the courts, the next time you see a kid eating a peach, you better ask her if she washed it very, very thoroughly first. Or maybe you should tell her to eat organic instead.

Pest Control's Best Bud: Representative Charles Stenholm (D-TX)

In June 1995 the industry magazine *Pest Control* published a list of 21 "friends" of the industry in Congress. "Think of it as a voting, complaining, check- and letter-writing guide the next time you're reminded that someone in Washington is out to get you," opined the magazine. Stenholm made the cut.

Indeed, Stenholm, a cotton farmer himself, has always been a friend to agribusiness. His seat on the House Agriculture Committee gives him sway over important federal agriculture policy. In the late 1980s, he supported proposed legislation that would have prohibited states from establishing stronger pesticide safety laws than the federal government. He supported early versions of the Food Quality Protection Act that eased regulations for the industry without including new protections for children and infants. He also sought to limit the EPA's power to phase out methyl bromide, a pesticide that contributes to depletion of the ozone layer.

But just because Stenholm is a friend to the pesticide industry doesn't mean he doesn't need buttering up like any other member of Congress. That's where the "check-writing" comes in.

Between 1991 and 1998, when Stenholm met Vice President Al Gore and convinced him to tell the EPA to slow down on pesticide review, the congressman collected $226,876 in PAC and large individual contributions from pesticide manufacturers and members of the Food Chain Coalition, an ad hoc industry group that lobbied Congress and the EPA to delay regulation of organophosphate and carbamate insecticides.

Sugar, Part of a Healthy Diet?

Is sugar good for you? How much should you eat? Hmmm . . . what do the government experts think? The United States Department of Agriculture (USDA) dietary guidelines issued in 2000 say that you should "choose beverages and foods to moderate your intake of sugars." Ok, but what did government experts want to say? An earlier draft of the dietary guidelines, following the advice of nutritionists, said that people should "choose foods and beverages to limit your sugars intake." But the Sugar Association didn't like the use of the word "limit." Neither did the National Soft Drink

Association, the Grocery Manufacturers Association, nor the National Confectioners Association and the Chocolate Manufacturers Association. "It goes to the very livelihood of our industry," Drew Davis, chief lobbyist for the National Soft Drink Association, told *Legal Times,* "Is it going to be the official nutrition policy of the government to discourage the consumption of our product?"

The pro-sugar lobby put on a full-force lobbying campaign, calling in chits with their friends in Congress. Senators Larry Craig (R-ID) and Kent Conrad (D-NE), the number 1 and number 4 recipients of sugar-daddy campaign contributions from 1995 to 2000 (with $71,602 and $44,726, respectively), circulated a letter to then–agriculture secretary Dan Glickman calling on him essentially to overrule the nutritionists' recommendation, citing rules that require any such change to be backed by "sound science"—a classic industry stratagem for blocking or delaying regulatory actions. According to a report in *Legal Times,* sugar industry lobbyists wrote the initial draft of the letter.

Ultimately, 30 Senators—22 Republicans and 8 Democrats, including several on the committee that oversees the Department of Agriculture's budget—signed the letter. This group received 40 percent more in contributions from the sugar industry than the average senator.

The result? When the USDA announced its revision of the federal food guidelines in May 2000, the nutritionists' language had been quietly dropped. Now they tell Americans to "moderate" their sugar intake. And the significance of this change isn't as fluffy as cotton candy. Among other things, the dietary guidelines regulate what the federal government, the nation's largest food buyer, can purchase for the more than 50 million people it feeds daily in the army, prisons, and schools.

The sugar lobby was less successful in the international arena in April 2003, when the World Health Organization (WHO) issued official diet recommendations. Despite pressure from big sugar, the agency recommended that people restrict intake of added sugar in their diet to 10 percent or less of the total calories they consume. But the fight isn't over. According to the industry newsletter *Food Chemical News,* Andrew Briscoe, president of the Sugar Association, threatened that the industry he represents would "exercise every avenue available" to discredit the report, including going to Congress to raise questions about U.S. funding of the agencies.

PART THREE

OUR ENVIRONMENT IS BEING DESPOILED

"I think there's no question that people are influenced by who they spend their time with. And unfortunately, given the way our political system is set up, our political system is based on private contributions. Where do private contributions come from? They can come from small people . . . but the large people understand that if they give a contribution of serious magnitude, that they will at least get access to make their case."

—Harold Ickes, White House Deputy Chief of Staff, 1994–1997, quoted on PBS's Frontline, October 1998

THE SECRET LIFE OF DICK CHENEY

When Vice President Dick Cheney was charged with developing an energy policy for America, he consulted with those he knew best— the energy industries that had been so generous to the Bush-Cheney campaign. But we don't know the whole story—Cheney is keeping it secret!

On January 29, 2001, just over a week after his inauguration, speaking in the cabinet room of the White House, President George W. Bush announced a meeting of a new energy task force, to be chaired by Vice President Dick Cheney. The president wanted a report on "how best to cope with high energy prices and how best to cope with reliance on foreign oil." That is, he wanted an account on the state of the energy crisis and what to do about it. The president said, "Can't think of a better man to run it than the vice president."

Dick Cheney, like his boss, is an oilman. He spent five years at the helm of the Dallas-based Halliburton Company, the world's largest oil service company (and now, a major contractor in the reconstruction of Iraq). He reportedly sold stock and options worth more than $30 million in compensation when he left the company in 2000 to serve as vice president. Even once he took up his new job, he continued to get income from Halliburton, receiving $367,000 in deferred salary payments in 2001 and

2002; in addition, he held 433,333 unexercised stock options in the company. Putting Cheney in charge of developing a national energy policy was a bit like putting Ted Nugent in charge of animal welfare.

In May 2001 Cheney delivered to the president a 170-page report with a nice blue cover, entitled *National Energy Policy*. Tucked in the report was recommendation after recommendation favoring the energy industry, while giving short shrift to environmental and public health concerns. (The month before, in a speech before Associated Press editors, Cheney had remarked that "conservation, while perhaps 'a sign of personal virtue,' does not make for sound or comprehensive [energy] policy.")

Cheney's task force report recommended drilling for oil in Alaska in the Arctic National Wildlife Refuge, weakening regulation for air pollution controls at power plants, increasing oil and gas exploration on public land, repealing a Depression-era law preventing national utility monopolies, expanding nuclear energy, building new refineries, and increasing reliance on coal.

How did the vice president arrive at all these great ideas? We don't know—it's a secret! This despite the sweeping nature of the task force recommendations, many of which soon found their way into regulatory rules and legislation.

During the months that Cheney's task force was deliberating, it held numerous meetings with energy industry lobbyists and officials to get their advice, a fact that leaked out while the meetings were under way. In response, Congressmen John Dingell (D-MI) and Henry Waxman (D-CA) asked Energy Department officials to supply them with information about the Energy Task Force and its meetings, pointing to a law known as the Federal Advisory Committee Act (FACA), which requires advisory committees to notify the public of their meetings. Those meetings must also be on the record, except under specific circumstances. But when the vice president's office wrote back, it was to reject the idea that the energy task force's meetings were subject to FACA. The VP also claimed that these meetings had included broad representation not just from the energy industry but also from conservation groups, academia, and Congress.

Meanwhile, the Natural Resources Defense Council (NRDC), an environmental group, had filed a Freedom of Information Act (FOIA) request asking for access to the energy task force's records. Again, the Bush administration refused to supply the information. So the NRDC went to court, and the following year, in March 2002, a federal judge ordered the Department

> * * * * *
>
> *"You can guarantee that the ones who contribute are going to get access, no question about that,"*
>
> —Representative Tom Bliley (R-VA), *quoted in* Speaking Freely, *2nd edition, CRP*

of Energy to release some 13,500 pages of documents relating to the task force. These records comprised just a portion of the task force's deliberations, since they do not include records from the vice president's office, or even all of the Energy Department's records. Even though the records that were supplied included large sections that were blacked out, the picture they revealed of industry involvement in the Cheney energy plan is overwhelming.

Overall, from January through September 2001, according to an analysis by NRDC, task force officials had 714 direct contacts with industry representatives and only 29 with nonindustry representatives.

What organizations were represented? They included the National Association of Manufacturers, the mammoth trade association whose members include ExxonMobil, Marathon Oil, and Arch Coal; the Nuclear Energy Institute; the Edison Electric Institute, the trade association for the utility industry; the National Mining Association; Westinghouse; the American Petroleum Institute, the lobby group for the oil and gas industry; and yes, Enron, among others.

As for conservation groups, they did not get nearly as much face time as the energy industry groups did. In mid-February, a coalition known as the Green Group requested a meeting with the vice president; they were denied. On February 20, the same group also requested a meeting with Energy Secretary Spencer Abraham; the secretary's scheduler told them that he was too busy. It wasn't until March 21, 2001, that a policy staffer, Margot Anderson, wrote an e-mail to another DOE staff member, asking him to contact representatives from environmental groups to get their policy recommendations and get them back to her within 48 hours. "Can you then review the proposals and recommend some we might like to support that are consistent with the Administration energy statements to date?" asked Anderson. Two days later, as reported by Public Citizen, Anderson wrote another e-mail, asking for comments on a new environmental chapter for the task force report. "I am unclear about the process on this one. I do know the topic was added in late," she says. While the Green Group did eventually get a meeting with the task force staff director, it was not until April 4, and lasted less than an hour.

Perhaps the amount of attention lavished on the industry groups at the expense of the environmental groups has something to do with their campaign contributions—or rather the lack thereof: environmental groups contributed $4.1 million to federal candidates and parties from 1999 through 2002, 10 percent to Republicans. Meanwhile, the companies and industry organizations that enjoyed extensive contacts with the Cheney task force were the source of $80.3 million in campaign contributions to federal candidates and parties from 1999 through 2002, two-thirds

THE ENERGY & NATURAL RESOURCES SECTOR AND THE 2004 PRESIDENTIAL CANDIDATES*

*Source: CRP; includes indiv ($200+) and PAC contributions

$3,019,900.....GEORGE W BUSH (R)

$92,800...JOHN KERRY (D)
$91,300...JOE LIEBERMAN (D)
$72,400...HOWARD DEAN (D)
$68,200...RICHARD A GEPHARDT (D)
$52,400...WESLEY CLARK (D)
$37,700...JOHN EDWARDS (D)
$29,300...BOB GRAHAM (D)
$12,000...CAROL MOSELEY BRAUN (D)
$10,500...DENNIS J KUCINICH (D)
$4,000...AL SHARPTON (D)

of that to Republicans, according to the Center for Responsive Politics.

Vice President Dick Cheney is still fighting to keep records of his energy task force as secret as possible. In December 2003 the U.S. Supreme Court agreed to hear the case brought by the conservative watchdog group Judicial Watch and the Sierra Club arguing that the Cheney Task Force was, indeed, subject to the federal law governing advisory committees. (Judicial Watch had brought a similar lawsuit against Hillary Clinton and her health care task force in the 1990s.) Justice Antonin Scalia caught flak in early 2004 for going on a duck-hunting trip with the vice president while the case was pending.

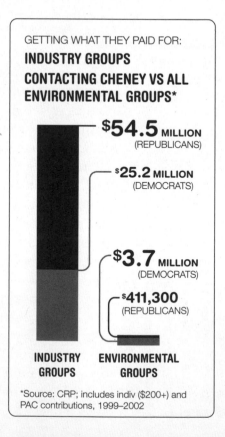

GETTING WHAT THEY PAID FOR:
**INDUSTRY GROUPS
CONTACTING CHENEY VS ALL
ENVIRONMENTAL GROUPS***

$54.5 MILLION
(REPUBLICANS)

$**25.2** MILLION
(DEMOCRATS)

$3.7 MILLION
(DEMOCRATS)

$**411,300**
(REPUBLICANS)

**INDUSTRY
GROUPS**   **ENVIRONMENTAL
GROUPS**

*Source: CRP; includes indiv ($200+) and
PAC contributions, 1999–2002

IT'S THE ENERGY TASK FORCE REALITY SHOW!
WITH YOUR HOST—DICK CHENEY!

CONTESTANT:

EDISON ELECTRIC INSTITUTE
(Electric Utilities)

PAID TO PLAY* (1999–2002):

$40,640,900

— REPUBLICANS 67%
— DEMOCRATS 33%

What they wanted:
Weakened air pollution controls for coal-burning power plants, known as "New Source Review"

What the Cheney Energy Task Force Report gave them:
"The NEPD Group recommends that the President direct the Administrator of the Environmental Protection Agency, in consultation with the Secretary of Energy . . . to review New Source Review regulations."

Summary of winnings:
Internal agency reviews completed; EPA issued new regulations essentially exempting coal-burning utilities from installing pollution control devices when making upgrades; regulations being challenged in court (see chapter 12)

But why stop there? They also wanted:
Repeal of the Public Utility Holding Company Act (PUHCA), a Depression-era law designed to protect utility ratepayers by preventing the formation of national monopolies

What the Cheney Energy Task Force Report gave them:
"The NEPD Group recommends that the President direct the Secretary of Energy to propose comprehensive electricity legislation that . . . repeals the Public Utility Holding Company Act."

Summary of winnings:
Repeal of PUHCA incorporated into energy legislation pending in Congress

They knew they were on a roll now . . .

Edison Electric Institute (Electric Utilities)—paying $40,640,900–continued . . .

They also wanted:

Clean Air Act eased by promoting market-based trading emissions system that environmentalists say will increase air pollution by 21 million tons over ten years

What the Cheney Energy Task Force Report gave them:

"The NEPD Group recommends that the President direct the EPA Administrator to work with Congress to propose legislation that would establish a flexible market-based program to significantly reduce and cap emissions of sulfur dioxide, nitrogen oxides, and mercury from electric power generators."

Summary of winnings:

In February 2002 President Bush announced "Clear Skies" Initiative; after legislation to implement stalled in Congress, in December 2003 EPA proposed regulations accomplishing many of same goals

CONTESTANT:

NUCLEAR ENERGY INSTITUTE
(Nuclear Energy, subset of electric utilities)

What they wanted:

Expansion of nuclear power; tax breaks

What the Cheney Energy Task Force Report gave them:

"The NEPD Group recommends that the President support the expansion of nuclear energy in the United States as a major component of our national energy policy . . . [and] support legislation clarifying that qualified funds set aside by plant owners for eventual decommissioning will not be taxed as part of the transaction."

Summary of winnings:

Tax breaks for nuclear industry incorporated into energy legislation pending before Congress

CONTESTANT:

COAL INDUSTRY

PAID TO PLAY* (1999–2002):

$7,379,342

— REPUBLICANS 88%

— DEMOCRATS 12%

What they wanted:

Money for "Clean Coal" government programs and tax incentives criticized by environmental groups as taxpayer giveaways

What the Cheney Energy Task Force Report gave them:

"[T]he NEPD Group recommends that the President direct the Department of Energy to continue to develop advanced clean coal technology by: investing $2 billion over 10 years to fund research in clean coal technologies; supporting a permanent extension of the existing R&D tax credit."

Summary of winnings:

Subsidies for clean coal technology in energy legislation pending in Congress

What they wanted:

Weakened air pollution controls for coal-burning power plants; Clean Air Act eased

See "Electric Utilities" for what the Cheney Energy Task Force Report gave them and a summary of their winnings.

CONTESTANT:

AMERICAN PETROLEUM INSTITUTE
(Oil and Gas Industry)

PAID TO PLAY* (1999-2002):

$59,125,974

— REPUBLICANS 79%

— DEMOCRATS 20%

What they wanted:
Opening Arctic National Wildlife Refuge (ANWR) for drilling
What the Cheney Energy Task Force Report gave them:
"The NEPD Group recommends that the President direct the Secretary to work with Congress to authorize exploration and, if resources are discovered, development of the 1002 Area of ANWR."
Summary of winnings:
Attempts to include drilling in Arctic National Wildlife Refuge in energy legislation pending in Congress

But why stop there?

They wanted:
Executive order that requires federal agencies to "include in any federal action that could significantly and adversely affect energy supplies, distribution, or use, a detailed statement . . ."
What the Cheney Energy Task Force Report gave them:
"The NEPD Group recommends that the President issue an Executive Order to direct all federal agencies to include in any regulatory action that could significantly and adversely affect energy supplies, distribution, or use, a detailed statement . . ."
Summary of winnings:
Executive Order 13211 issued May 18, 2001, "Actions Concerning Regulations that Significantly Affect Energy Supply, Distribution, or Use"

*Source: CRP; includes indiv ($200+), PAC, and soft-money contributions 1999–2002 to federal candidates and parties

WHY JOHNNY CAN'T BREATHE

While asthma cases among children across the country have been doubling, electric utility lobbyists were making sure that the Cheney Energy Task Force exempted dirty coal-powered plants from laws requiring them to reduce pollution.

Fourteen-year-old Johnathan Sanders, a student at Martin Luther King Jr. Middle School in southeast Atlanta, suffered from asthma. So did more than 100 of his classmates, reported the *Atlanta Journal-Constitution* in February 2001. The school made as many as a dozen 911 emergency calls the previous year, and had one of the worst attendance histories of any school in the system. Sanders himself had missed seven days of school because of an asthma attack. The kids at King were not an anomaly either in Georgia or nationally. Statewide, 210,000 kids suffered from asthma, and they missed half a million school days a year because of the disease, according to a joint study released at Sanders's school by the American Lung Association of Georgia and the state Department of Human Resources. Nationwide, asthma cases have nearly doubled in the last two decades.

There is much research being done on the causes of asthma and why the disease is now more prevalent among kids. Air pollution is clearly a major culprit, scientists say. Kids are more vulnerable to air pollution than adults because their lungs are bigger compared to their bodies; pound-for-pound, children breathe 50 percent more air than adults do. That means they breathe in more pollution, too. Some 1.2 million kids live within 30 miles of any one of a dozen coal-fired power plants in Georgia, and coal-powered plants are particularly pernicious polluters, emitting arsenic and mercury, along with a long list of other chemicals. Coal-fired plants are a major source of air toxics, emitting 96 percent of the electric industry's sulfur dioxide, 93 percent of nitrogen oxide, 88 percent of carbon dioxide, and 99 percent of mercury.

> ★ ★ ★ ★ ★
>
> *"It's a new kind of campaign organizing. It's not getting out the vote, it's getting out the money."*
>
> —*John Endean, a lobbyist for the American Business Conference, describing George W. Bush's network of big-money bundlers known as Pioneers,* American Lawyer *magazine, July 26, 1999.*

One month after the *Atlanta Journal-Constitution* reported on Georgia's burgeoning asthma problem, a lobbyist for the Southern Company, whose subsidiary, Georgia Power Company, operates coal-fired plants in the state, sent an e-mail to Joseph Kelliher, then an official with the U.S. Department of Energy. Kelliher represented the energy secretary's office on Vice President Cheney's energy task force.

"Good morning," the lobbyist, Michael Riith, wrote Kelliher. "This is the document I told you was in 'the works' on NSR in relation to the national energy strategy. . . . I hope this is helpful. After talking with you yesterday, the last thing you need is another issue to deal with. Thanks for your consideration. Again, I look forward to lunch on Tuesday." Attached to the e-mail was a document detailing all the changes the Southern Company wanted to "NSR," or New Source Review, the Environmental Protection Agency's (EPA) program requiring old power plants making upgrades or building new facilities to install new pollution-reduction technology.

Why did the Southern Company want these changes? Flash back to November 1999, when the Justice Department under President Clinton had sued Southern and six other electric utilities in the Midwest and South for failing to install pollution control technology when they revamped older power plants. The legal action targeted 51 power plants in 10 states that the Justice Department charged had exposed the public to tens of millions of tons of sulfur dioxide, nitrogen oxides, and particulate matter.

According to an EPA consultant, the violations at the power plants in question were to blame for as many as 9,000 premature deaths and 120,000 asthma attacks every year, and bringing the plants into compliance would have reduced air pollution by nearly 7 million tons annually—half of all the electric utility air pollution produced by power plants in the country.

The Southern Company and the other utilities faced the possibility of paying significant civil penalties, of up to $27,500 per plant per day. The Southern Company was not pleased, and neither was the rest of the electric utility industry. The Edison Electric Institute, the lobby arm for the utility industry, decried the EPA for following a "revisionist view of history," arguing they had to do upkeep on their plants just to keep them running for customers. But the industry was not going to rely on the courts to hear their side of the argument. By the time the Justice Department announced the lawsuits, the industry was already powering up for the 2000 elections, funneling campaign contributions to the nascent Bush campaign.

In May of 1999 Edison Electric Institute president Thomas Kuhn, who had been a Yale classmate of then-candidate George W. Bush, sent a letter to potential contributors to the campaign on Bush campaign stationery. "[Bush campaign fundraisers] have stressed the importance of having our industry incorporate the [electric utility] tracking number in your fundraising efforts. . . . It does ensure that our industry is credited, and that your progress is listed among the other business/industry sectors." Kuhn became a Bush "Pioneer." He wasn't the only one: Anthony Alexander, president of FirstEnergy, also one of the companies targeted in the Justice Department lawsuits, was a Pioneer, too. Former Republican National Committee chairman Haley Barbour, also a Pioneer, represented the Southern Company and another utility lobby group, the Electric Reliability Coordinating Council (ERCC). The Southern Company's PAC, its executives, and their families contributed $366,790 to the Bush campaign, the RNC, and the Bush inaugural, according to watchdog group Public Citizen in an investigative report. The electric utility industry contributed nearly $445,000 to Bush's 2000 campaign (and had kicked in more than $737,000 toward his 2004 race). Overall, electric utilities have given more than $86 million to federal candidates and parties since 1989.

So by the time Southern Company lobbyist Riith wrote his e-mail in 2001 suggesting that the Cheney task force recommend changes to the EPA's New Source Review program, the company was already cozy with the new administration. Indeed, throughout their deliberations, task force members met with the Southern Company at least seven times and the Edison Electric Institute at least 14

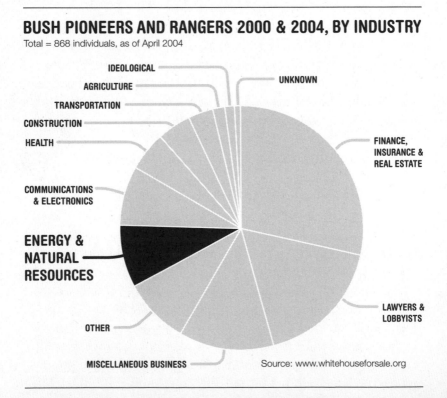

BUSH PIONEERS AND RANGERS 2000 & 2004, BY INDUSTRY
Total = 868 individuals, as of April 2004

IDEOLOGICAL

AGRICULTURE

TRANSPORTATION

CONSTRUCTION

HEALTH

COMMUNICATIONS & ELECTRONICS

ENERGY & NATURAL RESOURCES

OTHER

MISCELLANEOUS BUSINESS

UNKNOWN

FINANCE, INSURANCE & REAL ESTATE

LAWYERS & LOBBYISTS

Source: www.whitehouseforsale.org

times, according to documents uncovered by the Natural Resources Defense Council (NRDC) [see chapter 11]. Task force members also met with two other utility companies facing lawsuits by the Justice Department, Cinergy and FirstEnergy, as well as lobbyists representing all of the companies facing lawsuits.

When the Energy Task Force released a formal report with recommendations in May 2001, the Southern Company's suggestions were embedded within it. The EPA and the Energy Department were asked to review the New Source Review regulations, and the Justice Department was ordered to analyze whether its lawsuits against the utilities were "consistent" with the law. Two weeks before the report was published, Haley Barbour donated $250,000 to an RNC fundraiser, $150,000 of which came from the Southern Company, according to Public Citizen.

In June 2002 the EPA issued recommendations on changes to the air pollution regulations, and the following year, in October 2003, the new regulations became final. The industry got all it wanted, and then some. The crux of the air pollution program—limiting how much change a utility could make to its plants before triggering the requirement to install stronger pollution controls— was essentially eviscerated. Utilities would be able to make hundreds of millions of dollars worth of changes to their plants without triggering the requirement to install better pollution controls.

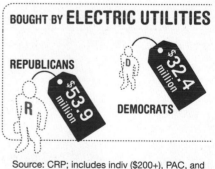

BOUGHT BY **ELECTRIC UTILITIES**

REPUBLICANS

$53.9 million

$32.4 million

DEMOCRATS

Source: CRP; includes indiv ($200+), PAC, and soft-money contributions 1989–2004 to federal candidates and parties

Finally, the new regulations obviously threatened the lawsuits that the Justice Department had already filed. What power would Justice Department attorneys have to get utilities to the settlement table if most of the changes made by the utilities that were being challenged would be completely legal under the new regulations? Indeed, it didn't take long after the EPA issued the new regulations on air pollution for the DOJ to start backing off.

A coalition of environmental and public health groups filed a lawsuit in October 2003 challenging the new regulations, as did attorneys general from 14 states and the District of Columbia; that legal action is now winding its way through the courts. Back in Georgia, far away from Washington, D.C., and the maneuverings there, there is still an asthma problem for kids. The local American Lung Association chapter recently announced a newly updated "Open Airways for Schools" program for kids with asthma, particularly poor kids, who tend to go untreated.

RETURN OF THE TOXIC AVOIDERS

Polluting companies are leading the fight in Congress to avoid paying for the toxic waste they have left behind at sites across the country. Resulting funding cuts have led to a reduction in cleanup efforts nationwide by nearly 50% since the late 1990s. Apparently it's cheaper for polluters to pay off politicians than to clean up their own mess.

For more than seventy years, until filing for bankruptcy in 1986, Continental Steel Corporation near downtown Kokomo, Indiana, a city of 46,000 people, produced nails and wire from scrap metal. The plant also produced plenty of pollution. PCBs, metals, lead, and other toxic chemicals were found on and near the 183-acre site, contaminating groundwater and the nearby Wildcat Creek. These chemicals have serious health effects for humans. People who are exposed to lead can develop nerve disorders, memory problems, and high blood pressure. Children are at a higher risk because their growing bodies absorb more lead. They often suffer from slow growth and behavior problems. PCBs are linked to cancers, as well as damage to the nervous and immune systems.

In 1989 the U.S. Environmental Protection Agency (EPA) designated Continental Steel as an official Superfund site. In the years following, progress was made on cleaning up the worst of the pollution. The agency hauled away nearly 2,500 barrels of chemicals from the site. Nearby residents whose lawns were contaminated with lead saw the dirt dug out and replaced with new sod. A chain-link fence with barbed wire was put up around the site, keeping people from entering the contaminated area.

Then the funding dried up, and cleanup work ground to a stop.

Superfund is the law established by Congress in 1980 to clean up the nation's worst toxic waste sites—relics of a time when less was known about the harm that chemicals could do. The arsenic, lead, mercury, cadmium, DDT, chlordane, benzene, and other nasty chemicals that have leached into groundwater and soil have caused fish and wildlife to sicken and die and has threatened human life.

One in four Americans lives within four miles of a Superfund toxic waste site, and more than 10 million of them are children. Kids who are born to parents living within one-quarter of a mile of a toxic waste site are at a greater risk for birth defects.

From its inception, the program has operated under the principle that the "polluter pays." The concept is as simple as "clean up your own mess." The companies responsible for the pollution—not the taxpayers—are supposed to shoulder the cost of cleanups. The EPA determines which companies are "potentially responsible" for pollution at a specific site. These companies, in turn, can seek funds from other companies or groups that also contributed to the contamination to a lesser degree. To cover costs of cleaning up sites where polluters cannot be determined or are no longer in existence, Congress also set up the Superfund Trust Fund, funded by taxes on the oil and chemical industries.

Since 1995, however, Congress has refused to reauthorize the taxes on the oil and chemical industries—the source of more than $213 million in campaign contributions since 1989. From a high of $3.6 billion in 1995, the Superfund

BOUGHT BY **OIL & CHEMICAL INDUSTRIES**

REPUBLICANS

$158.6 million

R

$54 million

DEMOCRATS

Source: CRP; includes indiv ($200+), PAC, and soft-money contributions 1989–2004 to federal candidates and parties

THEY GAVE MONEY. THEY GOT VOTES. COINCIDENCE?

OIL AND CHEMICAL COMPANIES WANTED THE SENATE TO VOTE AGAINST REINSTATEMENT OF THE SUPERFUND TAX.*

Senators who said:

SURE! got **$138,300**†

Senators who said:

NOPE! got **$37,200**†

*108th Congress, 1st session, Senate Vote # 97, 43Y-56N, N=Industry position
†Average received, 1999–2004

Trust Fund budget has dwindled to nearly nothing. In that time, polluting corporations have avoided paying more than $10 billion in Superfund-related taxes, what amounts to a $4-million-a-day tax break, according to U.S. PIRG.

Although Presidents Ronald Reagan, George H. W. Bush and Bill Clinton all supported the use of these taxes, President George W. Bush, the recipient of more than $4.4 million from oil and chemical industries for his presidential campaigns, opposes it. Instead, the president supports effectively increasing the amount paid by taxpayers. The result: taxpayers now pay 79 percent of the costs of Superfund cleanups, and polluters only 21 percent, a complete flip-flop from 1995, when polluters paid 82 percent of the costs and taxpayers, 18 percent. Over the past decade, the program funding has declined by 35 percent.

Back to Continental Steel in Indiana. Despite the fact that there is still plenty more that needs to be done to clean up the site—dredging the creek beds,

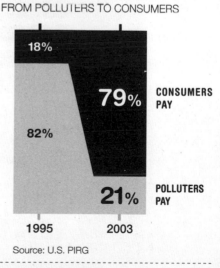

SHIFTING THE COST OF CLEANUP
FROM POLLUTERS TO CONSUMERS

18%

79% CONSUMERS PAY

82%

21% POLLUTERS PAY

1995   2003

Source: U.S. PIRG

for example, where there is still a ban on eating fish because of PCB contamination—the site received no cleanup funds whatsoever in fiscal year 2002 or 2003. Another ten sites nationwide, ranging from New Hampshire to Texas to Oregon, also got no funding in fiscal year 2003. Funding cuts have led to a reduction in the rate of cleanup nationwide for Superfund sites by nearly 50 percent since the late 1990s, from an average of 87 sites per year to just 42 sites in 2002.

"I feel abandoned," Carolyn Kauble, who lives one block away from the Continental Steel site, told the *New York Times*. Before he died, her husband, a former employee at Continental Steel, was one of the local activists who worked hard to bring attention to the pollution problems there. "It's not completed. It's not done. It's

---

TOXIC AVOIDERS ON THE LOOSE!

A blandly named group of companies, the Superfund Settlements Project Coalition, led the successful fight against a March 2003 proposal to reinstate taxes on the oil and chemical industries to help pay for the Superfund program. **All are major campaign contributors—and major polluters!**

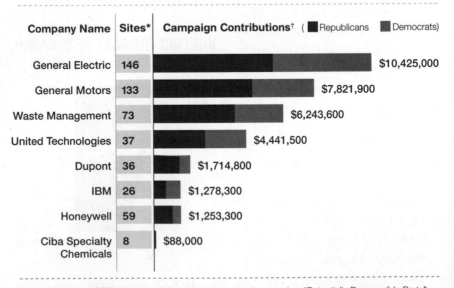

Company Name	Sites*	Campaign Contributions† (■Republicans ■Democrats)	
General Electric	146		$10,425,000
General Motors	133		$7,821,900
Waste Management	73		$6,243,600
United Technologies	37		$4,441,500
Dupont	36		$1,714,800
IBM	26		$1,278,300
Honeywell	59		$1,253,300
Ciba Specialty Chemicals	8		$88,000

Sources: EPA and CRP *Number of sites where company is named as "Potentially Responsible Party"
†Includes indiv ($200+) and PAC contributions to federal candidates and party committees, 1989–2004.

---

not safe," she added. Another nearby resident, John Rawlings, told the *Times*, "They carried the ball to the 90-yard line. They have to carry it 10 more yards that are the toughest part, and they backed off."

Why doesn't Congress do something to rescue Superfund? In March 2003 Senators Frank Lautenberg (D-NJ) and Barbara Boxer (D-CA) tried. They cosponsored an amendment that would have reinstated the Superfund Tax and forced polluters to pay for toxic cleanup. It failed, 56 to 43. The senators who voted to reinstate the tax received, on average, $138,300 in campaign contributions from oil and chemical companies over the previous six years, while the senators who said no received $37,200.

* * * * *

"I'm not claiming to be a Boy Scout. No question I thought what I was doing was in the best interests of my clients."

—*Gordon Gooch, lobbyist for energy and oil interests, who sat in Representative Tom DeLay's (R-TX) office and drafted a government moratorium on environmental and safety regulations that was passed by the House of Representatives at the beginning of 1995, the* Washington Post, *March 12, 1995*

RIGGED CONTEST: HUMMER VERSUS HYBRID

Requiring cars and especially SUVs to get more miles to the gallon is the single biggest step we could take to curb the greenhouse gases that contribute to global warming. Congress, however, has said "no" to strengthening fuel economy standards, under pressure from intense lobbying and millions of dollars in campaign contributions from the auto industry and union.

The next time you are stuck in a traffic jam on your way home from work, think about this. Every car emits 70 tons of carbon dioxide into the atmosphere over its lifetime, and SUVs are even more prolific, emitting about 100 tons. In fact, every gallon of gas you burn off in your car pumps 28 pounds of carbon dioxide into the atmosphere. All told, cars and "light trucks" (including SUVs) emit a whopping 20 percent of the nation's carbon dioxide emissions, according to the Sierra Club.

You can't see carbon dioxide, and you can't smell it, but it is one of the major greenhouse gases contributing to global warming. Sea level has risen by 10 inches in the past century, and the 10 hottest years on record have all occurred since 1980. In the European Alps, glaciers are half as large as they were in 1900. In Alaska, the Columbia glacier has retreated more than eight miles in sixteen years. Ironically, companies exploring for oil there are increasingly foiled because warming temperatures are thawing the tundra, making travel with heavy equipment difficult.

All this might seem abstract, as you sit with your engine idling, wondering if you will make it home in time to join your kids for dinner, but the consequences of a warmer earth are anything but theoretical. Warmer temperatures mean more bugs, and more bugs means the spread of more illness. Recent outbreaks of the West Nile virus in New York and Colorado have been linked to unusually mild winters, which infected larvae are able to survive. Since 1990 there have been outbreaks of malaria in California, Florida, Georgia, Michigan, New Jersey, and New York. The International Panel on Climate Change (IPCC), a United Nations organization made up of 2,500 scientists from around the world, predicts that global warming will increase the percentage of the world population at risk of infection by 20 percent. Warmer temperatures also bring a greater danger of hurricanes and droughts, putting people's lives in danger and also threatening wildlife.

The car or SUV you are driving, however, doesn't need to be such a big polluter. If federal fuel economy standards were raised to 45 miles per gallon for cars and 34 miles per gallon for SUVs, not only would carbon dioxide be cut by 600 million tons, but consumers would also save at least $45 billion a year at the gas pump.

But it is no accident that fuel economy standards (known as CAFÉ, for Corporate Average Fuel Economy) have not risen to meet their technological potential since they were enacted in 1975, in the midst of the OPEC oil embargo. During the first 10 years of the program, CAFÉ requirements for cars doubled. However, the target of 27.5 miles per gallon for cars, set for 1985, remains the standard more than 15 years later.

Meanwhile, SUVs have always gotten special treatment. When the CAFÉ law was first enacted, a different standard was set for "light trucks," which then represented less than 20 percent of the market and were largely used in construction and farming. Light trucks only needed to meet a standard of 20.7 miles per gallon (very recently raised slightly to 22.2 miles per gallon for the 2007 model year).

Then came the SUV explosion. Weighing enough to be classified as "light trucks," the Ford Explorers, Toyota Highlanders, and GMC Yukons, not to mention the Hummers and the Chevrolet Suburbans, became ubiquitous on the nation's highways, making up nearly half of the new vehicle market in 2003—and probably a good proportion of your daily traffic jam.

In the mid-1990s, when the Transportation Department announced that it was considering raising fuel efficiency standards for light trucks by as much as 40 percent, the auto industry swung into action, with help from the United Auto Workers (UAW) union. While the auto industry, the source of more than $90 million in campaign contributions since 1989, devotes three-fourths of its largesse to Republicans, the UAW, which on most issues, such as trade and worker safety, takes stances opposed to industry, has given 94 percent of the $19.5 million it has contributed since 1989 to Democrats.

In November 1995, at the behest of Representative Tom DeLay (R-TX), who has received over a quarter of a million dollars from the auto industry during his years in office, Congress blocked the Transportation Department from using any agency funding for the work required to raise CAFÉ standards. This became an annual ritual, with Congress repeatedly ordering the agency not to develop new CAFÉ rules. The ties between DeLay and the auto industry only grew over the years—in 2001, the Alliance of Automobile Manufacturers Inc. hired one of his former top aides, Tony Rudy. DeLay ranks fourth in the House of Representatives for contributions from the industry.

BOUGHT BY **AUTOMOTIVE INDUSTRY**
REPUBLICANS — R — $66.8 million
DEMOCRATS — D — $23.1 million

BOUGHT BY **AUTO UNION**
REPUBLICANS — R — $198 Thousand
DEMOCRATS — D — $18.3 million

Source: CRP; includes indiv ($200+), PAC, and soft money contributions 1989–2004 to federal candidates and parties

In 2002 Senators John Kerry (D-MA) and John McCain (R-AZ) proposed to raise CAFÉ standards to 36 miles per gallon for cars and light trucks by 2015. Soon advertisements were on the airwaves and in the newspapers inside the Beltway and in several rural states, largely sponsored by the Coalition for Vehicle Choice, a group including General Motors, DaimlerChrysler, Ford, and a major dealers association, reported *National Journal's* Peter H. Stone. One spot declared that families would have to use compact cars to haul their snowmobiles. Another featured a small business owner who said that he and his truck were "joined at the hip" and that if Congress adopted the new standards, it would put "both of us out of business." Auto companies also went on a lobbyist-hiring frenzy, securing the help of the likes of John Breaux Jr., the son of Senator John Breaux (D-LA).

The Kerry-McCain proposal was no match for this lobbying blitz. In March 2002 the Senate voted 62 to 38 to adopt a different amendment, by Senators Carl Levin (D-MI) and Kit Bond (R-MO), then the number 4 and number 18 lifetime recipients of campaign contributions from the auto industry, which merely told the Department of Transportation to study the issue. "In a nearly evenly divided Senate, when labor breaks with the Democrats, it's almost impossible for the Democratic-environmentalist position to prevail," Larry Sabato, a government professor at the University of Virginia told *National Journal.* "Some liberal Democrats are so closely aligned with labor that they're not going to turn their backs on a union on a bread and butter issue."

Indeed, you might say that legislation to raise fuel economy standards is stuck in a Congressional traffic jam. The sad difference between the fate of CAFÉ bills and you, also stuck in a jam, is that eventually, you will get out of yours.

A Hummer of a Tax Break

Buried in President Bush's tax bill that was signed into law in May 2003 was a provision that on its face seemed innocuous. Small businesses and self-employed people are now allowed to deduct up to $100,000 (previously, it was $25,000) for the purchase of new equipment, including any vehicle the IRS considers to be a truck,

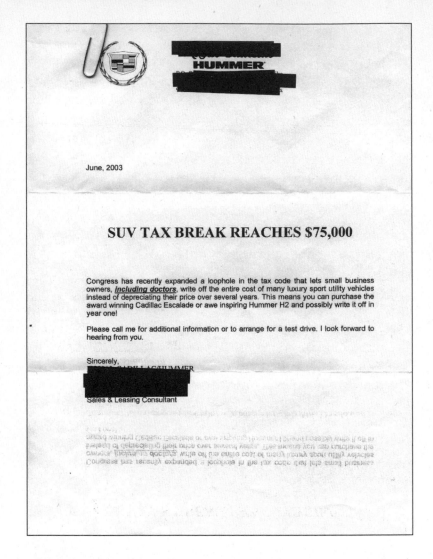

June, 2003

SUV TAX BREAK REACHES $75,000

Congress has recently expanded a loophole in the tax code that lets small business owners, **_including doctors_**, write off the entire cost of many luxury sport utility vehicles instead of depreciating their price over several years. This means you can purchase the award winning Cadillac Escalade or awe inspiring Hummer H2 and possibly write it off in year one!

Please call me for additional information or to arrange for a test drive. I look forward to hearing from you.

Sincerely,

Sales & Leasing Consultant

which is a vehicle weighing 6,000 pounds or more. No sooner did the law change than dealers selling Hummers and other large SUVs meeting the weight requirement started dangling the tax break in front of potential customers. Car dealers have contributed $42.7 million to federal campaigns since 1989, according to the Center for Responsive Politics, 75 percent to Republicans. In the letter from a New Jersey dealership reprinted here, which was sent to a local doctor, the headline is actually wrong—while the original proposal by President Bush put the tax break at $75,000, Congress tacked on another $25,000.

The Hummer H2—which Arnold Schwarzenegger brags about helping GM design before he ran for governor of California—weighs more than three tons and gets about 11 miles per gallon.

★ ★ ★ ★ ★

PREVARICATOR

"I will go to Sacramento and I will clean house. As you know, I don't need to take money from anyone. I have plenty of money myself."

—**Arnold Schwarzenegger** *announcing his candidacy for California governor on the* Tonight Show with Jay Leno, *August 2003*

"Special interests have a stranglehold on Sacramento. Here's how it works: Money comes in, favors go out. The people lose. We need to send a message. Game over. If you want to change this state, then join me."

—**Arnold Schwarzenegger,** *in a 30-second TV ad for his campaign, September 2003*

"I get donations from business and individuals, absolutely. They're powerful interests who control things."

—**Arnold Schwarzenegger** *on the more than $1 million he had raised from companies and individuals with business before the state, at the beginning of September 2003. Ultimately, he raised over $22 million for his campaign, of which $4.8 million came from his own pocket and $4.5 million came in the form of a loan from a major state bank, which was later ruled illegal. Much of the rest came from real estate, high-tech, and entertainment business interests, including Bush '04 Ranger/'00 Pioneer Alex Spanos, who along with his family members gave Schwarzenegger $227,200; Bush '04 Pioneer Jerry Perenchio, the CEO of Univision, who together with his wife gave $42,400 (along with over a $1 million earlier to support Schwarzenegger's 2002 after-school program ballot initiative); Bush '04 Ranger Elliott Broidy, owner of a capital management firm, who gave him the individual maximum of $21,200; Bush '04 Pioneer Robert Day, owner of a private money management firm, who gave him $21,200; Bush '04 Pioneer Bob Tuttle, an auto dealer, who gave him $21,200; and Bush '04 Pioneer Dwight Decker, CEO of an electronics company, who gave him $21,200.*

How much exactly is unsure, because the manufacturer, GM, doesn't report the figures to the government. The H2 is so big it isn't required to meet any fuel economy standards, although the Transportation Department's National Highway Transportation Safety Administration has proposed bringing them into the fold. Schwarzenegger was promised the first H2 off the assembly line. "Look at those deltoids," the former bodybuilder said as he fondled the vehicle's sheet metal at a promotional event in New York's Times Square. "Look at those calves."

PART FOUR

OUR SAFETY IS BEING JEOPARDIZED

"Whose fundraiser was I at last night? I can't even remember. You go to so many of these things that you don't remember."

—Ken Montoya, lobbyist for the National Air Traffic Controllers Association, speaking to a reporter during a fund-raising breakfast for Representative Nick Rahall (D-WV) in May 1997.

THE HOMEGROWN CHEMICAL WEAPONS THREAT

Despite the September 11 terrorist attacks, and warnings from top government authorities that chemical plants in the U.S. are priority targets, there are still no mandatory federal security standards for chemical facilities. Instead, the powerful industry has so far blocked attempts by Congress and the EPA to impose tough rules, insisting that its voluntary safeguards are enough.

Six months after the September 11 terrorist attacks, reporter Carl Prine of the *Pittsburgh Tribune-Review* decided to find out for himself how well chemical plants in his area were protected from intruders. Wearing a press pass and carrying a camera, Prine strolled unhindered through 30 sites, walking in broad daylight up to tanks, pipes, and control rooms without ever being stopped by security guards or other workers.

Not far from Pittsburgh, at a warehouse in Forward Township owned by Vopak, a leading chemical distributor, he spent more than an hour on-site without being accosted, even climbing on top of chemical tanks, rail cars, and crates storing tons of highly toxic chlorine. Vopak's warehouse is one of at least 123 plants nationwide where an accident or attack involving lethal chemicals stored on-site could endanger more than one million people living nearby, according to records filed by the companies themselves with the Environmental Protection Agency. There are another 700 facilities where a "worst-case" release could threaten more than 100,000 people.

Over the next two months, Prine visited another 30 chemical factories, shippers, and warehouses in Baltimore, Chicago, and Houston. He found "safeguards so lax that a potential terrorist can easily reach massive tanks of toxins that endanger millions." Not only could a stranger enter unmolested, personnel on-site often gave him directions to the most sensitive valves and control rooms! More than half the plants had "no noticeable [security] cameras, fences or locks at all," he reported.

"I began to wonder, I mean, what would it take for me to get arrested at one of these plants?" Prine later recounted. "Would I have to come in carrying an AK-47?"

For all the talk about terrorists getting their hands on chemical weapons overseas, huge stocks of highly dangerous and accessible chemicals are already right here at home. An April 2000 study by the Justice Department concluded that "the risk of terrorists attempting in the foreseeable future to cause an industrial chemical release is both real and credible," noting that it would be far easier than constructing a weapon of mass destruction. In February 2003 the Bush Administration warned that terrorists "may attempt to launch conventional attacks against the U.S. nuclear/chemical industrial infrastructure to cause contamination, disruption and terror. Based on information, nuclear power plants and industrial chemical plants remain viable targets."

But while nuclear power plants are already subject to tough federal security requirements, there are no mandatory federal security standards for chemical plants. The $450 billion chemical industry insists that voluntary safety programs promulgated by the American Chemistry Council (ACC), a

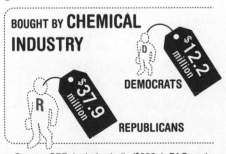

BOUGHT BY **CHEMICAL INDUSTRY**

$12.2 million — DEMOCRATS

$37.9 million — REPUBLICANS

Source: CRP; includes indiv ($200+), PAC, and soft-money contributions 1989–2004 to federal candidates and parties

trade association, are sufficient to reduce hazards and improve security at their plants. It's an argument that was successfully used by the airline industry to thwart congressional attempts to regulate airport security operations, that is, until September 11th changed the political dynamic. And despite Prine's shocking reports, which were reconfirmed in a *60 Minutes* exposé in November 2003, and vigorous efforts by environmental groups like Greenpeace, as of early 2004 the industry—which has given over $50.1 million to federal candidates and parties since 1989—was still having its way.

It's not as if Congress was completely indifferent to the problem. In October 2001, while the ruins at Ground Zero were still smoldering in lower Manhattan, Senator Jon Corzine (D-NJ) introduced a modest bill called the Chemical Security Act. It would have explicitly given the Environmental Protection Agency the authority to regulate security at the approximately 15,000 chemical facilities around the country. It would have also required them, where "practicable," to use inherently safer technologies and thus reduce the amounts of dangerous chemicals they store on-site. (Such alternatives do exist—for example, a sewage treatment plant in the Washington, D.C., area has ended its use of ultrapoisonous chlorine gas, replacing it with a safer alternative.)

At first Corzine's bill seemed to be on track to passage. On July 25, 2002, it was approved with only minor modifications by the Senate Environment and Public Works Committee by a vote of 19–0. Corzine was hopeful that his proposal would be included in pending legislation to create the Department of Homeland Security. But then the chemical lobby swung into action.

The American Chemistry Council rallied a coalition of trade associations and conservative think tanks, including the American Petroleum Institute and groups representing agribusiness, mining, trucking, and utilities. The ACC claimed that Corzine's bill would lead to "government micromanagement" of the industry. It also opposed giving the EPA authority to oversee industry security efforts, fearful the agency would be too tough. And it insisted that its self-imposed safety code was adequate, even though it barely covered 1,000 plants and was not enforceable.

As Common Cause pointed out in a report, by early September

six Republican senators on the Environment and Public Works committee—Kit Bond (R-MO), Mike Crapo (R-ID), James Inhofe (R-OK), Bob Smith (R-NH), Arlen Specter (R-PA), and George Voinovich (R-OH)—had publicly changed their minds about the bill they had earlier voted for, claiming the bill "misses the mark" and could "hurt our nation." They were joined by Senators George Allen (R-VA) and Richard Shelby (R-AL), who also criticized the bill.

At this point, a little money-in-politics scorecard becomes handy, since Senator Corzine was up against some of the chemical industry's most loyal and well-compensated allies in the Senate.

CHEMICAL INDUSTRY SCORECARD
SENATOR CORZINE AND THE OPPOSITION

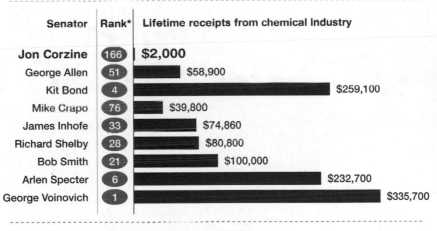

Senator	Rank*	Lifetime receipts from chemical Industry
Jon Corzine	166	$2,000
George Allen	51	$58,900
Kit Bond	4	$259,100
Mike Crapo	76	$39,800
James Inhofe	33	$74,860
Richard Shelby	28	$80,800
Bob Smith	21	$100,000
Arlen Specter	6	$232,700
George Voinovich	1	$335,700

* Rank among colleagues for receipts from chemical industry
Source: CRP; includes indiv ($200+) and PAC contributions, 1989–2004

Oops, we almost forgot to mention another key industry ally who chimed in with a well-timed June 20 letter to Tom Ridge, then the homeland security czar, to keep chemical security away from the EPA and put it in his new agency, whose formation was then still being debated.

| Billy Tauzin | 4 | $158,797 |

Contributions to Representative Tauzin (R-LA) from the chemical industry spiked sharply upward the month after he sent Ridge that letter, hitting $6,460—his best month of the whole 2001–2002 election cycle. And an analysis of the industry's overall contributions month-by-month shows a vivid correlation with its efforts to block Corzine's bill. As the timeline below shows, chemical cash erupted in October 2002, just as the industry's congressional allies were keeping the Corzine proposal from being added to pending legislation to create the Department of Homeland Security.

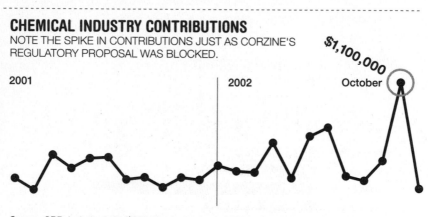

CHEMICAL INDUSTRY CONTRIBUTIONS
NOTE THE SPIKE IN CONTRIBUTIONS JUST AS CORZINE'S
REGULATORY PROPOSAL WAS BLOCKED.

$1,100,000

2001   2002   October

Source: CRP; includes indiv ($200+), soft-money, and PAC contributions to federal candidates, party committees and leadership PACs

While interventions by these members of Congress were effectively killing the Corzine bill, the chemical lobby was also operating on a parallel track against the EPA. Documents leaked to Greenpeace and obtained by the group through a Freedom of Information Act request show that the agency was looking forward to tackling chemical plant security, a responsibility it was delegated under President Bush's original homeland security plans. Mandatory rules were drafted and a speech was written for then–EPA administrator Christine Todd Whitman in which she promised to send EPA representatives to high-priority chemical facilities starting in July 2002.

But the speech was never given. Why not? "We heard from industry," a former EPA official told Anne-Marie Cusac, who wrote about the issue for *The Progressive* magazine. "We would oppose anything from the EPA that would slow down the strong efforts currently in place addressing security," an ACC spokesman declared.

And so, the Corzine bill and the EPA's tentative efforts to address chemical plant security were blocked. By October 2002 the agency had publicly disavowed any intention of setting security standards, and Whitman told reporters that the Bush administration was inclined to support a new bill being drafted by Senator Inhofe. That bill puts responsibility for monitoring the chemical industry's compliance in the hands of the Department of Homeland Security, does not require the use of inherently safer technology, and spells out no minimum standards for improved site security. (Whitman stepped down from running the EPA in May 2003, saying she wanted to spend more time with her family.)

> * * * * *
>
> *"Having to call people up and ask for money is inherently demeaning."*
>
> —*Senator John Kerry,*
> Boston Globe, *May 16, 1997*

President Bush has done mighty well by the chemical industry, by the way. Eight individuals connected to the industry were "Pioneers" in 2000. One, Frederick Webber, was then the president of the American Chemistry Council. Bush has appointed several friends of the chemical lobby to top government positions, including three of the five members of the Chemical Safety and Hazard Investigation Board, an independent federal agency entrusted with investigating chemical accidents. And the industry has returned the favors, giving him over $1.3 million since 1999.

As for those "strong efforts currently in place addressing security" promoted by the ACC, Carl Prine and *60 Minutes* discovered in the fall of 2003 that not enough had changed from his first jaunt around some of the nation's most sensitive chemical facilities. Rail cars full of chlorine gas, corrosive enough to dissolve human teeth, stood unguarded on tracks not far from Pittsburgh. Broken fences and unlocked gates gave him easy access to tanks holding 20 tons of chlorine. Prine slipped through a fence hole into a Giant Eagle grocery warehouse where workers chatted with him about the

Please Return Your Elected Officials to an Upright Position

After TWA Flight 800 crashed in 1996, President Clinton promised to toughen airport security measures, declaring that all flights entering or leaving the United States would be searched before takeoff—"Every plane, every cabin, every cargo hold, every time." But it didn't happen. A presidential commission chaired by Vice President Al Gore called on the Federal Aviation Administration to stop allowing airlines to hire baggage-screening companies based solely on who was the lowest bidder and insisted on criminal background checks for all airport employees. Tragically, as we now know, had the Gore Commission's original recommendations been followed, the September 11 hijackers might never have been able to get past airport security that fateful day. But fierce opposition from the Air Transport Association (ATA), which feared that longer lines at security checkpoints would turn off passengers, managed to block any implementation of these proposals.

As Jim Hall, then the chair of the National Transportation Safety Board and a member of the Gore Commission, told Public Citizen, "The rules got all diluted."

The Gore Commission had also originally proposed that all bags be matched to passengers, to prevent terrorist attacks like the Lockerbie bombing of Pan Am flight 103. On September 5, 1996, it took a strong position, insisting that this be implemented on domestic flights within 60 days. Two weeks later, Gore withdrew that proposal, writing the ATA a conciliatory letter. A day after that, large soft-money contributions starting flowing from the airlines to various Democratic committees: $40,000 from TWA, $265,000 from American Airlines, $120,000 from Delta, $115,000 from United, $87,000 from Northwest, according to a CRP analysis done for the *Boston Globe*. By Election Day, these totaled $585,000—more than double what the airlines gave Democrats in the same period before Gore's letter.

Even after the September 11, 2001, terrorist attacks, safety measures are being watered down at the behest of this powerful lobby. On December 15, 2003, President Bush signed a four-year $60 billion aviation bill that includes $14 billion for construction projects, $2 billion for bomb-screening machines, and allows cargo pilots to carry guns. When the bill passed the House and Senate, each chamber had included a provision requiring the airlines to provide mandatory security training for flight attendants. The flight attendants' union pushed hard for that provision. Patricia Friend, its president, complained that "two years after the September 11 attacks, the nation's flight attendants have not received any meaningful anti-terrorist security training." Friend added, "The pilots, even the few who have guns, are under strict orders not to leave the cockpit . . . and air marshals are only onboard selected flights. In most cases, the flight attendants and passengers are left defenseless in the cabin."

But, as with so many dirty deals in Congress, something happened to the bill when it was taken up in a conference committee. Due to the intervention of House Republican leader Tom DeLay (R-TX), acting at the behest of Continental Airlines (which is based in his district), the bill now leaves it to the discretion of the TSA and the White House to decide whether such training is necessary. In addition, say the flight attendants, Republicans on the conference committee worked with the airlines "to make flight attendant security training completely voluntary—and paid for by the flight attendants."

This provision, along with others that would privatize some air traffic control towers and open some domestic routes to foreign carriers, caused all the Democrats on the conference committee to refuse to sign on to the final version of the bill. Since 1989, the airlines have given $26 million to federal candidates and parties. Until 1996, that money was almost evenly divided between the parties, with Democrats receiving slightly more. But since 2000, over 60 percent of it has flowed to Republicans.

Pittsburgh Steelers while he checked out a 20,000-pound tank of anhydrous ammonia. "No one stopped him as he touched train derailing levers, waved to security cameras, and photographed chlorine tankers and a nitric acid vat" at the Sony Technology Center in Westmoreland County, the *Pittsburgh Tribune-Review* reported.

"We might as well face the fact that security at a 7-Eleven after midnight is better than that at a plant with a 90-ton vessel of chlorine," John DePasquale, a former Georgia-Pacific security chief, told Prine. "A guy with a suitcase full of explosives can kill tens of thousands of people, and we're not doing anything about it."

OF KILLER PENS AND AK-47S

You might feel safer if everybody who bought a handgun went through a background check first—but thanks to the National Rifle Association and other gun rights groups, which have poured millions of dollars into political campaigns, commonsense gun control measures languish in Congress.

It looks like a pen. But it's not a pen. Pull it open and the bottom half, where you'd think the ink should be, becomes the barrel of a gun. The top half, bent at a 90-degree angle to the barrel, becomes the gun's grip. You are now armed with the "only legal pengun in the world," manufactured by Stinger Manufacturing Company, which offers you a "whole new world of possibilities," according to the company's Web site.

While federal law requires purchasers of "gadget-type firearms and 'pen guns' which fire fixed ammunition" to undergo extended background checks, receive approval from local police, and to register the weapon, the Stinger pengun is subject to none of these conditions. With a stroke of a real pen, the kind with ink, U.S. Attorney General John Ashcroft could require Stinger buyers to meet these requirements. In fact, in this post-9/11 age of orange alerts and homeland security, you would think he would be doing just that. But instead the Bureau of Alcohol, Tobacco, and Firearms (BATF), under his leadership, says the pengun is more like a standard handgun because in order to be fired, the grip must be angled to its barrel. If you are buying a regular old handgun, the gun safety laws are far less stringent.

The attorney general, who made the cover of the National Rifle Association (NRA) magazine back in July 2001, has also benefited from more than $619,000 in direct contributions and independent expenditures and communications costs by the gun rights groups and individuals during his career in the Senate. While he served in Congress, Ashcroft voted against gun safety legislation 13 out of 13 times, according to the Brady Campaign To Prevent Gun Violence, including votes against proposals that would have required child safety locks on guns and imposed stricter regulation of firearm purchases at gun shows.

According to the University of Chicago's nonpartisan National Opinion Research Center, nearly 79 percent of the public believe that a police permit should be required for purchasing guns. Large majorities also favor restricting individual gun purchases to no more than one a month and requiring safety training for gun purchasers. Three-fourths support mandatory registration for handguns. Surely popular opinion is due to the endless death toll:

The United States has the dubious honor of having the highest rate of homicide and suicide by gun among developed countries, and guns are the leading cause of death for people ages 10 to 24. In 2001 alone, nearly 30,000 people died from gun wounds.

Yet none of these overwhelmingly popular gun control proposals are law, primarily because Congress and the administration regularly capitulate to the tough lobby of the NRA and other gun rights groups. Together these groups have contributed $17.2 million since 1989 to federal political campaigns, 85 percent to Republicans. In contrast, gun control groups have contributed just $1.6 million over the same time period, 94 percent to Democrats, according to the Center for Responsive Politics.

Over the past 25 years, the gun lobby has shot down numerous attempts to regulate guns. The NRA has beaten off proposals to require chemical "tags" in explosives, which would make them

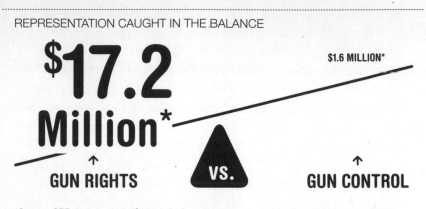

REPRESENTATION CAUGHT IN THE BALANCE

$17.2 Million*

$1.6 MILLION*

↑
GUN RIGHTS

VS.

↑
GUN CONTROL

*Source: CRP; includes indiv ($200+), PAC, and soft-money contributions to federal candidates and parties, 1989–2004

easier to trace in preventing terrorism; it has successfully opposed the ban of "cop-killer" bullets designed to pierce body armor. The gun group has thwarted proposals to require gun locks on guns, or to put limits on how many guns can be purchased per month. The list goes on and on.

To appreciate the firepower of the gun lobby, flash back to 1999. In April, twelve students and a teacher died at Columbine High School in suburban Colorado, after they were shot by students Dylan Klebold and Eric Harris. All four guns they used were purchased by an 18-year-old friend at Denver-area gun shows from private sellers who are not required to run background checks on buyers the way that gun shops must under the 1993 federal Brady Law. "I wish a law requiring background checks had been in effect at the time," the friend, Robyn Anderson, later testified before the Colorado legislature. "I don't know if Eric and Dylan would have

---

Test Your Money-in-Politics IQ

What is the leading cause of death among children among those listed below?

a. Cancer   b. Pneumonia   c. Influenza   d. HIV/AIDS   e. Gunfire

Answer: e. More children die from gunfire in this country than by a, b, c, and d combined.

been able to get guns from another source, but I would not have helped them."

In the aftermath of the tragedy, Congress considered legislation to require background checks for gun show purchases. Not once but twice the Senate voted against this commonsense measure. The 44 senators who said no to strong background checks over the course of a week in May 1999 were the beneficiaries, on average, of nearly 29 times more campaign cash from gun rights groups than the 40 senators who said yes to background checks on three votes—$23,340 versus $815. (These amounts include independent expenditures and communications costs made on behalf of members, in addition to direct campaign contributions. The NRA is notorious for using independent expenditures. The law allows organizations to spend unlimited amounts of money on advertisements and other electioneering materials supporting or opposing a candidate, so long as they do not coordinate these activities with the candidate.)

The Senate finally approved a bill requiring a three-day waiting period for gun purchases, but only because then–vice president Al Gore broke a tie. Their colleagues in the House disagreed. The 212 House members who voted the NRA's way on two separate roll call votes were the beneficiaries of 31 times more campaign cash from gun rights groups than the 189 members who voted in favor of

---

THEY GAVE MONEY. THEY GOT VOTES. COINCIDENCE?

THE NRA WANTED TO KEEP SALES AT GUN SHOWS LEGAL WITHOUT BACKGROUND CHECKS.*

Senators who said:
SURE! got **$23,340**[†]

House members who said:
SURE! got **$11,195**[†]

Senators who said:
NOPE! got **$815**[†]

House members who said:
NOPE! got **$355**[†]

*106th Congress, 1st Session, Senate vote #111, 51Y–47N, Y=gun rights position; Senate vote #118, 48Y–47N, Y=gun rights position; Senate vote #134, 50Y–50N, N=gun rights position. 106th Congress, 1st Session, House vote # 234; 218Y–211N, Y=gun rights position; House vote #235; 193Y–235N, N=gun rights position [†]Source: CRP; averages include indivs ($200+), PAC, and independent expenditures and communications costs on behalf of candidates, 1995–2000 for senators, 1997–2000 for House members

background checks—$11,195 versus $355. The measure never became law, because the House and Senate couldn't agree on a final version. You can go to a gun show today and buy a gun from a private seller without going through a background check.

Another issue looming on the NRA's horizon is the ban on assault weapons. Federal law now bans the purchase of assault weapons such as AK-47s, Uzis, and TEC-9s, which have the capacity to hold as much as 50 rounds of ammunition. The NRA has long opposed the ban. In 1996, then-representative Bob Barr (R-GA), a board and lifetime member of the NRA, orchestrated a successful vote, 239 to 173, to repeal the assault weapon ban. Because the Senate didn't act, the ban still stands, but on September 13, 2004, the law is due to expire. High on the NRA's to-do list: to make sure that it doesn't get renewed.

Top on the NRA's list, however, is another matter, closer to the gun industry's wallets: getting gun manufacturers, dealers, and importers off the hook from civil lawsuits filed by victims of gun crimes. In recent years, victims of firearm violence have gone to the courts, arguing that those who make and sell guns should have some responsibility for crimes committed with them. Legislation to protect the gun industry from consumers wielding lawsuits nearly passed Congress early in 2004. In the House, Representative Cliff Stearns (R-FL), recipient of $30,550 in direct campaign contributions from gun rights groups during his career in the House, was the sponsor. Senator

* * * * *

"Met with [blank] from the National Rifle Association. He showed me the piece the National Rifle Association is going to send out hitting [blank]. God, is it tough . . . I cannot tell you how tough it is!—They are going to send it to 90,000 members. And he said if he has enough money he's going to send it out to 100,000 Oregon gun owners, or something like that."

—*Diary entry of former senator Bob Packwood (R-OR), dated October 6, 1992, as reported in "The Buying of the Congress," Center for Public Integrity. Packwood later tried to sanitize the entry, perhaps because it appears to refer to potentially illegal coordination between the NRA and his campaign on an independent expenditure.*

Larry Craig (R-ID), a board member of the NRA since 1983, and the third top recipient of NRA direct contributions in the Senate since 1989, with $45,439, sponsored the Senate version.

But the legislation, which was considered to be a shoo-in for passage (indeed the House did approve it), hit a snarl in the Senate when gun control advocates successfully attached two amendments. The first would have required background checks on weapons buyers at gun shows. The second extended the ban on assault weapons due to expire in September 2004. Senator Craig found these additions so objectionable that he argued against passage of his own bill, saying it had been "so dramatically wounded it should not pass." With the NRA urging defeat, the Senate voted overwhelmingly against the legislation.

A few days later, one of his colleagues, Senator George Allen (R-VA) remarked,"I'm constantly amazed about how we in the Senate spend so much time accomplishing so little." The Senate had spent nearly a week debating the bill.

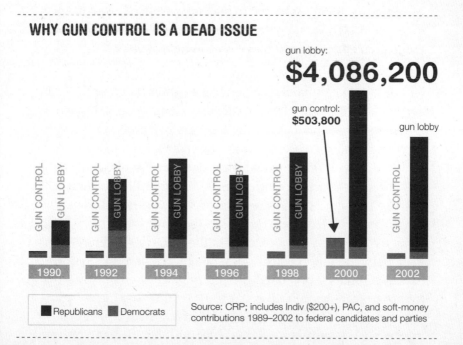

WHY GUN CONTROL IS A DEAD ISSUE

gun lobby:
$4,086,200

gun control:
$503,800

gun lobby

1990   1992   1994   1996   1998   2000   2002

■ Republicans ■ Democrats

Source: CRP; includes Indiv ($200+), PAC, and soft-money contributions 1989–2002 to federal candidates and parties

HOW LONG CAN YOU "STUDY" A PROBLEM BEFORE IT GOES AWAY?

The link between repetitive injuries like carpal tunnel syndrome and shoulder tendinitis and the workplace has long been established. Big business interests, which outspent labor unions on campaign contributions 14-to-1 in the 2000 elections, want the government to keep studying the problem endlessly rather than issue tough regulations against these preventable injuries.

On the face of it, it hardly seemed like a matter for controversy. In late January 2004, the National Advisory Committee on Ergonomics, a committee chartered by the secretary of labor, hosted a symposium on how repeated physical activities lead to workplace injuries. The committee would use the proceedings from the symposium, said the department's news release, to make recommendations to advance "OSHA's agenda of reducing the incidence of Musculoskeletal Disorders (MSDs) in the workplace."

But a controversy it was. Eleven of the country's leading experts in ergonomics—the science of designing workplace environments to reduce injury—boycotted the meeting. They complained that the government had already spent plenty of time and money studying the issue, and had already concluded that yes, repetitive injuries such as carpal tunnel syndrome and shoulder tendinitis are widespread in the workforce, and that yes, measures could and should be taken to reduce these types of injuries. These conclusions were drawn by a panel of 19 experts in fields such as biomechanics, orthopedics, and quantitative analysis who spent two years studying the issue, at the specific request of Republican opponents of ergonomics regulations in Congress, under the aegis of the National Academy of Sciences (NAS). The resulting study, published in 2001, found that some one million people lose time from work each year because of these types of injuries, and that some $50 billion in work-related costs is lost annually, about 1 percent of the entire gross domestic product. (Indeed the NAS had come to similar conclusions in a report published in 1998, and before that, in 1997, the National Institute for Occupational Safety and Health had as well.)

The boycotting scientists portrayed the OSHA (Occupational Safety and Health Administration) symposium not as an earnest attempt to understand the problem, but rather as a devious way to postpone action. "If enough people get up and say, 'We need to know more, we need to know more,' we'll end up

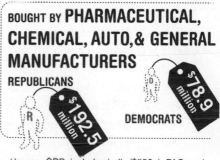

BOUGHT BY PHARMACEUTICAL, CHEMICAL, AUTO,& GENERAL MANUFACTURERS

REPUBLICANS

$192.5 million

$78.9 million

DEMOCRATS

Source: CRP; includes indiv ($200+), PAC, and soft-money contributions 1989–2004 to federal candidates and parties

with another comprehensive review," Don Chaffin, a University of Michigan industrial engineer, told the *Baltimore Sun*. Chaffin, one of the boycotters, added, "It's called paralysis by analysis." Another scientist compared the ergonomics controversy to that over tobacco decades before, when industry-influenced scientists delayed government action by endlessly debating whether tobacco really did, in fact, cause cancer.

Indeed, some of the most powerful interests in the country have opposed stronger ergonomics regulations for years—the U.S. Chamber of Commerce, the National Association of Manufacturers, and the National Association of Wholesaler-Distributors, just to name a few. While these organizations give some political money directly, the true magnitude of their power is reflected in their vast membership. For example, pharmaceutical, chemical, auto, and general manufacturers have contributed more than $272 million to federal candidates and parties since 1989.

Back when the first George Bush was president, his labor secretary, Elizabeth Dole, announced that OSHA would develop a worker safety standard on ergonomics. A long list of industry groups, generous campaign contributors all, objected. When OSHA began drafting regulations in 1995, Congress started passing amendments to funding bills prohibiting the agency from working on them. In 1995, 1996, and 1998, OSHA was forbidden to work on ergonomics. In 1999 the agency proposed regulations. The following year, in the waning days of the Clinton administration, OSHA issued regulations covering 102 million workers at 6.1 million work sites. The agency estimated that this would help workers avoid 460,000 injuries yearly, and that businesses would save some $9 billion a year.

> * * * * *
>
> *"Motivated and involved donors must enlist the support of family members to make contributions. As long as the money is under the control of a spouse or child and the check is drawn from their account, the contribution is deemed to come from the spouse or child. . . . No one should deprive the family of a vacation just to donate to candidates, but political contributions are probably worth at least as much as a glass of wine a week, another silk blouse, or a round of golf."*
>
> —Advice to donors from the Business Industry Political Action Committee, the country's first business PAC

While labor unions cheered, big business was outraged. Suddenly the meetings of the National Coalition on Ergonomics, an industry group opposing the ergonomics rule, got extremely crowded.

"There were 50 lawyers in the room and 20 on the phone," one source told the *Washington Post*. Stephen Bokat, general counsel of the U.S. Chamber of Commerce, told the paper, "All of the industry groups are meeting and working together. It's practically every association in town."

Big business always enjoys a heavy advantage over labor when it comes to campaign contributions, but the difference was even starker after President George W. Bush took his oath of office. Overall, in the 2000 elections, businesses outspent labor unions 14 to 1 on campaign contributions to federal candidates and parties, according to the Center for Responsive Politics. (These powerful interests did not limit themselves to campaign contributions. The U.S. Chamber of Commerce, for example, spent $25.5 million on issue ads, on a variety of concerns. This is advertising that stops just short of advocating the defeat or election of candidates. The AFL-CIO committed $21.1 million for the same.)

Once President Bush was in office, and both chambers of Congress were controlled by the GOP, business interests clearly had the advantage. Sure enough, one of Bush's first agenda items was ergonomics. The White House, worried about legal challenges if it simply revoked the regulation, turned to Congress, reported the Center for Responsive Politics. In late February of 2001, in a meeting between Bush and Republican congressional leaders, the decision was made to use a legislative procedure that had never been invoked before, the Congressional Review Act of 1996, which gives Congress 60 days to reject federal regulations. The Republican-controlled House and Senate voted to rescind the ergonomics regulations, and on March 20, 2001, President Bush signed the legislation. Scott Vinson, a lobbyist for the National Council of Chain Restaurants, and a former employee of the Chamber of Commerce, described the successful fight to overturn ergonomics regulations "a great example of the business community coming together."

The Bush Administration went on to announce a new ergonomics plan that would emphasize voluntary guidelines and educational efforts over strict requirements. In March 2003 the administration issued the first set of these types of guidelines, aimed at the nursing home industry. Industry associations were full of praise, but Service Employees International Union (SEIU) president Andrew L. Stern complained, "There is no incentive for employers to follow the guidelines, only excuses for not following them." OSHA's administrator, John L. Henshaw, was careful to say that the new guidelines were strictly voluntary. "There will not be enforcement," he declared to the *Washington Post*.

In addition, the administration formed a new National Advisory Committee on Ergonomics to advise OSHA—the same committee that sponsored the symposium in 2004 boycotted by leading ergonomics experts. Members of the committee include Willis Goldsmith, who worked on ergonomics at the U.S. Chamber of Commerce; James Koskan, director of risk control for Supervalue, a Minneapolis-based supermarket chain has been cited by OSHA for ergonomic violations; and Dr. Morton Kasdan, a hand surgeon who testifies for employers in worker compensation cases and has argued that injuries are often caused by depression. "By and large, everyone on the committee was selected because of their opposition to the ergonomic standard," David Rempel, a bioengineer with the University of California, who organized the boycott, told the *Baltimore Sun*. Despite the boycott, the meeting went on as planned.

The UPS Connection

Virtually the entire business community opposes strong ergonomics regulations. One the staunchest enemies of regulation over the years, however, has been United Parcel Service (UPS), with its thousands of brown-uniformed employees lifting and straining all day. Some 20,480 workers at truck services like UPS miss a day or more of work annually because of back, leg, and other musculoskeletal injuries. When OSHA was developing regulations, UPS flacked its own internal study denying the relationship between back injuries and loading packages. That didn't stop the company, however, from developing its own extensive ergonomics program in an attempt to prevent injuries among employees.

"This is the company that claims that ergonomics interventions do not prevent lifting-related injuries, but has held more than 20 workshops throughout the country to convey the importance of ergonomic principles, job set-up and methods, and workplace design," Eric Frumin, safety and health director for the labor union UNITE, pointed out in Senate testimony.

Nevertheless, the company remains adamantly opposed to federal regulations, and has contributed some $16 million to federal candidates and parties since 1989, 63 percent to Republicans, with special attention to lawmakers who champion the company's interests.

TOP RECIPIENTS OF UPS CAMPAIGN CONTRIBUTIONS
AND HOW THEY RETURNED THE GESTURE

RANK	NAME	TOTAL CONTRIBUTIONS	WHAT THEY DID FOR UPS
1	Anne M. Northup (R-KY)	$61,000	sponsored bill to overturn ergonomics regulations
2	John Linder (R-GA)	$63,600	sponsored bill to overturn ergonomics regulations
3	Chet Edwards (D-TX)	$62,300	
4	Bob Clement (D-TN)	$59,500	voted to overturn ergonomics regulations
5	Jerry Lewis (R-CA)	$57,800	supported UPS's bid for federal approval for cargo flights to China
6	Paul E. Gillmor (R-OH)	$56,100	voted to overturn ergonomics regulations
7	Nick Rahall (D-WV)	$55,800	
8	Henry Bonilla (R-TX)	$54,300	sponsored amendments in mid-1990s preventing OSHA from working on ergonomics rules
9	Don Young (R-AK)	$52,000	voted to overturn ergonomics regulations
10	John Boehner (R-OH)	$51,700	voted to overturn ergonomics regulations

Source: CRP; includes indiv ($200+) and PAC contributions 1989–2004; and thomas.loc.gov, news reports

PART FIVE

OUR RIGHTS
ARE BEING ABRIDGED

"Money is not the root of all evil in politics. In fact, money is the lifeblood of politics."

—**House Majority Leader Tom DeLay (R-TX),** Congress Daily, May 15, 1998

PARDON YOU?
IT DEPENDS

When a president gives special treatment to a billionaire fugitive like Marc Rich, who skipped town rather than face charges on tax fraud and trading oil illegally with Iran, we have to ask whether this country truly follows the principle of "liberty and justice for all." Perhaps the Pledge of Allegiance should end with the phrase "liberty and justice, particularly for those with money, connections, and plenty of campaign contributions."

America, the land of the free, imprisons more people per capita than any other country in the world. For every 10,000 Americans, 70 make their home in prison, six times the incarceration rate of the early 1970s, according to The Sentencing Project. This increase is primarily due to changes in sentencing policies, such as mandatory minimum sentences and "three strikes and you're out" laws, not any leap in the crime rate. In fact, while crime rates have declined in the last decade, the prison population has only grown. Today, there are some two million prisoners nationwide.

That load got a little lighter on January 20, 2001. That is when outgoing President Bill Clinton, as one of his last official acts, pardoned 140 people, ranging from Patricia Hearst Shaw to his half-brother Roger Clinton to Henry G. Cisneros, a former secretary of housing and urban development. But the pardon that drew the most raised eyebrows was for Marc Rich, a fugitive commodities trader indicted in 1983 for tax and wire fraud and trading oil illegally with Iran, who fled to Switzerland rather than face those charges. Rich, whose businesses are valued at $30 billion, was represented by Jack Quinn, former White House counsel, who (for a reported $400,000 fee) pled his case at the highest level, he told the media, after U.S attorney Mary Jo White gave him the "back of the hand" on the matter, refusing to consider it.

Rich's ex-wife, the songwriter and New York socialite Denise Rich, was a major donor to the Democratic Party. She has given more than $1 million to federal Democratic candidates and party committees since 1993. In the 2000 elections alone, she gave more than $375,000 to Democratic candidates and party committees, according to the Center for Responsive Politics, including $1,000 to Hillary Clinton's Senate campaign. She also donated $450,000 to President Clinton's presidential library foundation, gave $10,000 to his legal defense fund, and bought the First Family a set of coffee tables and chairs worth over $7,000.

Rich's relationship to President Clinton was so close that one of his first public appearances after the Starr Report came out in 1998 was at a fund-raiser at her New York apartment, which raised between $3 million and $4 million.

Denise Rich lobbied Clinton to pardon her former husband, writing to the president on December 6, 2000, "I am writing as a friend and an admirer of yours to add my voice to the chorus of those who urge you to grant my former husband, Marc Rich, a pardon for the offenses unjustly alleged and so aggressively pursued." Rich denied that her contributions had anything to do with her ex-husband's pardon. "Her political fund-raising and charitable activities have absolutely nothing to do with the pardon granted to her former husband," read a statement released by her publicist. Clinton said he pardoned Rich because he was convinced "on the merits" by Quinn, who had argued that Rich deserved a pardon because of his major philanthropy for Israeli charities and because other people who had executed similar tax schemes had escaped prosecution.

* * * * *

Bill Moyers: *"People with money should not be able to buy more democracy than people without money."*

Don Fowler, *then chair of the Democratic National Committee: "But they do, and we all know it. . . . Creating the opportunity to make your case through contributions is standard fare."*

—*Interview on PBS's* Frontline, *October 6, 1998*

For the families of the nation's prisoners, especially the 500,000 in prison for nonviolent drug offenses, however, it is hard to believe these denials would pass a laugh test. They know that they do not have the same sort of access to a presidential pardon that someone like Marc Rich does, with his high-level connections and deep pockets.

Interestingly enough, since 2000, Denise Rich has stopped giving campaign contributions to federal candidates! Could her interest in supporting Democrats have suddenly disappeared with the pardon of her ex-husband? (And in case you're wondering if we think only President Clinton favored big contributors with pardons, let us remind you of the first President Bush's pardon of financier Armand Hammer, for laundering illegal campaign contributions to President Richard Nixon, after he gave $200,000 to the Bush-Quayle Inaugural Committee and to the Republican National Committee.)

Prisons have become a $50 billion industry, and private prison companies dispense campaign contributions like anybody else vying to secure a government contract. In 1998 alone, private prison corporations and executives, companies such as Corrections Corporation of America, distributed more than $860,000 to candidates in 43 states, according to an analysis of campaign finance records by the National Institute on Money in State Politics. That total grew in 2000, when private prison companies gave over $1.1 million to candidates in just 14 southern states, the institute reported. In addition, private prison companies help fund the American Legislative Exchange Council (ALEC), a Washington, D.C.–based public policy organization that supports conservative legislators and lobbies for tough criminal justice legislation in the states. Tougher crime laws help keep the supply of prisoners up.

That fact hasn't escaped another group with an equally selfish interest in prison growth: prison guards' unions. None is more powerful than the California Correctional Peace Officers Association, which represents 31,000 current and retired prison officers. The California union spent almost $1 million in 1990 to elect "tough-on-crime" Republican Pete Wilson governor, and another million backing conservative candidates for the state legislature in 1992. Then it backed Proposition 184, the so-called "three strikes and you're out" initiative, which has led to more than 3,000 25-years-to-life sentences since then, half of which went to nonviolent offenders for crimes like drug possession, drug sales, and petty theft.

Not only have the California prison guards successfully invested in a vast expansion in the state's prison system; they've also gotten themselves some juicy rewards in their paychecks. Governor Wilson gave the union an 11 percent pay raise just before he left office in 1998. Then the union spent $2 million helping Democrat Gray Davis, a backer of "three-strikes-and-you're-out," win the governorship in 1998. In addition, it gave Davis another $1.4 million before he was recalled in 2003. He rewarded the union with pay hikes in 1999 and 2000. In 2003, with his back to the wall, Davis approved yet another salary increase for prison guards at the same time that the rest of his budget slashed state spending across the board. Overall, the union has spent at least $9.6 million on California politicians since 1998. At the federal level, private prison companies have given $1.6 million to federal candidates and parties since 1989. By contrast, there is no deep-pocketed lobby for prisoners and their families.

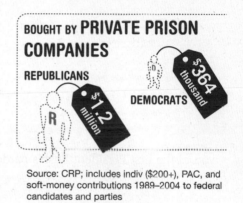

BOUGHT BY PRIVATE PRISON COMPANIES

REPUBLICANS
$1.2 million

DEMOCRATS
$364 thousand

Source: CRP; includes indiv ($200+), PAC, and soft-money contributions 1989–2004 to federal candidates and parties

Race, Crime, and Money

African Americans and Hispanics make up nearly 30 percent of the U.S. population, according to the 2000 census. But in that same year, 94 percent of all people prosecuted for using crack cocaine were either African American or Hispanic. This was despite the fact that out of a total population of 3.75 million crack users, only one-quarter were African American and less than 10 percent were Hispanic.

The racial disparity in who gets prosecuted for crack cocaine use gets even worse when you consider that when Congress enacted mandatory minimum sentencing laws in 1986, it decided that crack should be treated differently from powder cocaine, even though the two are chemically identical. The penalty for selling five grams of cocaine is five years in jail. For powder cocaine, you have to sell at least 500 grams (a little more than a pound) to trigger a five-year sentence. Thus, the penalty for crack is 100 times more punitive than for coke.

For years reformers in Congress have been trying to redress this imbalance, with little success. In 1995 the U.S. Sentencing Commission passed a guideline amendment to equalize the penalties, but Congress blocked its implementation. Every session of Congress since, Democratic New York Representative Charles Rangel has introduced legislation to reduce the penalty for crack cocaine to the same level as powder cocaine, but his bills have gone nowhere.

Now consider these elemental facts, drawn from our Color of Money report, which is covered in more detail in the primer that opens this book: Nine out of ten dollars over $200 contributed by individuals to federal campaigns and parties in the last two elections come from majority non-Hispanic white zip codes, yet nearly one out of three Americans is a person of color. One out of two of those dollars comes from a person living in a wealthy neighborhood. Dr. William E. Spriggs, executive director of the National Urban League Institute for Opportunity and Equality, says,

> Communities of color and the poor are severely underrepresented because of their inability to keep pace with the campaign contributions from wealthier, non-minority communities. The disparity underscores why legislators spend 100 hours on telecommunications reform and 10 hours on welfare reform.

Could it be that Congress prefers to treat people who buy powder cocaine—which is more expensive than crack and thus more likely to be bought by people of means—differently from people who buy crack, because Congress is more sensitive to the pain of well-off whites than it is to the pain of less-well-off people of color or ethnicity? You be the judge.

Ninety-nine Strikes and You're Still In

- Number of U.S. laws that expressly require the temporary suspension of government contractors from doing business with the government, if they are violated: 9
- Number of large government contractors that have ever been suspended or barred from receiving government business, 1990–2003: 2
- Names of those companies: General Electric and Boeing
- Number of criminal violations for which General Electric and Boeing have paid fines, 1990–2002: 99
- Date that Clinton Administration issued an anti-scofflaw rule that would have given federal contracting officials the authority to deny contracts to corporations that are repeat law-breakers: January 19, 2001.
- Date that the Bush Administration suspended implementation of that rule: January 20, 2001
- Number of states that penalize families, on the first violation, if a recipient of Temporary Assistance to Needy Families (TANF) refuses to engage in required work: 15
- Estimated number of families kicked out of the program from 1997 to 1999 because they refused to work or committed other violations: 540,000
- Total corporate tax welfare received by General Electric despite earning $51 billion in profits from 1996–2000: $12 billion
- Total cash welfare distributed to poor families in 2000 under the Temporary Assistance to Needy Families program: $10.8 billion
- Federal campaign contributions by General Electric, 1989–present: $10 million, 53% to Republicans
- Federal campaign contributions by Boeing, 1989–present: $8.3 million, 57% to Republicans
- Number of days a welfare recipient making the minimum wage would have to work in order to pay to attend a $1,000-a-plate fundraiser: 25

WHEN BIG BANKS HAPPEN TO LITTLE PEOPLE (PART 2)

Mega-campaign-contributing megabanks are pushing Congress and the feds to block strong state consumer laws protecting privacy and preventing predatory loans and other abusive practices. And they're winning. How would you like to see your social security number splashed across the city skyline?

On the morning of October 24, 2003, there it was, written in smoke high up in the sky for all in Midtown Manhattan to see: the first five digits of the Social Security number of Citigroup's CEO, Charles Prince. A California-based consumer group, the Foundation for Taxpayer and Consumer Rights (FTCR), had purchased it for just $30 on the Internet. The group had also bought the Social Security numbers of John Ashcroft, CIA Director George Tenet, and Federal Trade Commission Chairman Timothy Muris.

The California consumer group did the stunt for a reason. Ever since Congress repealed the Depression-era Glass-Steagall law in 1999, spurring a wave of mergers between banks, insurance companies, and securities firms, these new mega-financial institutions have been sharing personal information about their customers to better target their marketing. With your private information flying around in cyberspace, it's easy for companies, or apparently anybody with $30, to find out your Social Security number and other personal information, leaving you to scratch your head over why there are so many charges at Las Vegas casinos on your Visa bill. Indeed some 27.3 million Americans were victims of identity theft between 1998 and 2003, according to the Federal Trade Commission.

The California consumer group resorted to skywriting because Congress was about to make a decision on legislation to tighten up national privacy laws. The only problem was, this new law, while it would strengthen existing federal protections, contained a big bitter pill, which the banking industry, including Citicorp, was pestering Congress to prescribe: it would eliminate all state laws with tougher consumer protections. And it just so happened that California, in August 2003, had approved a law that was much stronger than the legislation pending in Congress.

The California law had not seen an easy road to passage. Gummed up in the statehouse the previous five years, the big banks gave in largely because supporters of the privacy law had garnered support for a ballot initiative that would have been even tougher. The new California law, signed by Governor Gray Davis as one of a flurry of bills he approved while facing recall, required

* * * * *

"In my two races for governor and last year when I ran for the Senate, I did it today's way. I locked myself in a room with an aide, a telephone and a list of potential contributors. The aide would get the 'mark' on the phone, then hand me a card with the spouse's name, the contributor's main interest and a reminder to 'appear chatty.' I'd remind the agribusinessman I was on the Agriculture Committee; I'd remind the banker I was on the Banking Committee. . . . I'd always mention some local project I had gotten—or hoped to get for them. Most large contributors only understand two things: what you can do for them or what you can do to them. I always left that room feeling like a cheap prostitute who'd had a busy day."

—*Senator Zell Miller (D-GA), op-ed in the* Washington Post, *February 25, 2001*

mega-banks to get permission from their customers before sharing information. At the time, John Ross, a Citigroup lobbyist, told the *American Banker* that "we were part of this and are pleased with the work done—it's a good fair result for everyone."

But were the big financial interests doing business in California all along banking on a "fix" from Congress? One has to wonder. After all, by the time Davis signed the bill in August, back in Washington, D.C., the House Financial Services Committee—whose 70 members collected an average of nearly $121,000 apiece in campaign contributions from the financial sector in the 2004 election cycle—had already voted, 63 to 3, to approve legislation that would override the California law. Congress was under great pressure to do something, because the 30-year-old federal Fair Credit Reporting Act was due to expire at the end of December. If they didn't renew the law, then there would be no federal standard at all, weak or strong. Were the banks thinking that they could get a better deal out of Washington than out of Sacramento?

It certainly looked that way to consumer advocates. In September, when the full House of Representatives approved the legislation, complete with the state-override, the vote wasn't even close—392 to 30. "I am not surprised because the banks and insurance companies have never been honest in this," Richard Holober, executive director of the Consumer Federation of California told the *San Francisco Chronicle*.

THEY GAVE MONEY. THEY GOT VOTES. COINCIDENCE?

THE FINANCIAL SECTOR WANTED CONGRESS TO REJECT A REQUIREMENT ALLOWING CONSUMERS TO "OPT OUT" FROM BANKS SHARING THEIR PERSONAL INFORMATION*

Senators who said:
SURE! got **$786,600**†

Senators who said:
NOPE! got **$576,600**†

*108th Congress, 1st Session, Senate Vote # 434, 70Y–24N; Y=Industry position
Source: †CRP; includes indiv ($200+) and PAC contributions, average received, 1999–2004

Meanwhile, California Democratic senator Dianne Feinstein made it clear she would fight to save her state's law. "What we have before the Senate is a very weak privacy standard—built for businesses at the expense of consumers—which legislatures in all 50 states are forever barred from improving," Feinstein said. On November 4, she offered an amendment that would have made the federal law as tough as the California law, allowing consumers to "opt out" so that financial services could not share their personal information. The amendment was tabled, by a vote of 70 to 24. Senators who voted in favor of the law received an average of nearly one-third more campaign contributions from the financial sector, versus senators who voted against it. By the end of the year, President George W. Bush signed the bill and it became law.

Loans Too Good to Be True

The story of Mrs. N., her name withheld to protect her privacy, a 72-year-old woman who has lived for more than 30 years in her home in Queens, New York, is all too typical of many of the nation's elderly. She was approached one day by a mortgage broker, who had noticed that she had a $2,200 tax lien on her house. The broker convinced Mrs. N. that she should refinance her house to pay her tax bill, and that this way she could get a lower interest rate than the 9 percent she was paying.

What Mrs. N. got instead was a $105,000 loan at 10.5 percent, which, because it was an adjustable rate, could climb even higher, to as much as 16.375 percent. Her monthly payments were higher by $200, and swallowed up two-thirds of her monthly income. The refinancing deal cost her nearly $11,000 in closing costs. All this, when she could have simply arranged an affordable payment plan with the New York tax office and paid off her back taxes that way. Mrs. N. couldn't afford to keep up with the loan and defaulted on it. She sought help with a local Legal Services office, whose lawyers are helping her under New York State laws that prohibit predatory loans.

Predatory lending is a huge problem not just for the elderly but also for African Americans and other communities of color. Banks target people who for one reason or another do not have good credit ratings, and sell them loans they cannot afford. They may charge them more interest than is necessary to compensate them for the increased risk they run; they may not take into account the ability of the person to repay the loan; or they may create such tough terms for the loan that it is nearly impossible for the person to meet their obligations. All of these kinds of loans can be considered "predatory," according to the National Community Reinvestment Coalition (NCRC). Many of these debtors are then forced into bankruptcy (See chapter 20). The NCRC has found that subprime loans (defined as loans offered above the prevailing interest rate, of which predatory loans are a subset) increase in a given neighborhood as the portion of African Americans and elderly increase.

Mrs. N. was able to get some help, but others in her situation may not anymore. You see, the bank that refinanced her loan was a subsidiary of a national bank. Under a new regulation issued in January 2004, by a U.S. Treasury Department agency, the Office of the Comptroller of the Currency (OCC), national banks are exempted from nearly all state consumer laws governing lending, checking accounts, and credit card company practices. Is this theme starting to sound more than a little familiar?

The OCC is not exactly a household word. What is this obscure agency, exactly, and why would it side with the big banks on the issue of preempting state laws protecting the elderly and minority communities from predatory lenders? Established in 1863, the OCC is the Treasury agency that regulates all national banks. The president appoints its director, who must be confirmed by the Senate. The current OCC director is John D. Hawke Jr., who was appointed by President Bill Clinton and began serving his five-year term in 1999. While Hawke had already been working for the Treasury Department, he had made his reputation as a top banking lawyer at Arnold & Porter, where he specialized in putting together banking merger deals.

Hawke hadn't had smooth sailing into his current position, however. Back in 1998, when President Clinton first proposed him for the OCC, his nomination was stalled for months by a group of Democratic senators led by Senator Paul Sarbanes of Maryland. The reason? Sarbanes charged that Hawke wasn't a strong enough supporter of the Community Reinvestment Act, the law that requires banks to give loans in low-income and minority communities—and which also provides protection against predatory loans. Sarbanes eventually relented, and Hawke won his confirmation. Of course, Hawke now works under the Bush administration, and the president has collected almost $39 million from the financial sector for his two presidential campaigns.

If the OCC's new regulation stands, then the State of New York could do nothing for somebody like Mrs. N. except refer her to the OCC's call center nearly 1,600 miles away in Houston, Texas. But according to Diana Taylor, superintendent of banks for the State of New York, who told Mrs. N.'s story at a hearing before the House Financial Services Committee in late January 2004, "it is not clear that this transaction would even be a predatory loan" under the new federal rules. Taylor charged, "[W]e have seen the OCC intervene time and time again on behalf of the nation's largest banks to prevent the implementation of state consumer protection laws. In these cases, the OCC has not been the consumer's advocate."

THERE ARE SOME THINGS MONEY CAN JUST KEEP TRYING TO BUY

Personal bankruptcies are at an all-time high. Contrary to conventional wisdom, the majority of people filing for bankruptcy are not frivolous spenders, but rather are victims of problems like job loss, medical problems, divorce, or separation. The banking and credit card industries are pouring millions into politicians' coffers, pushing legislation to make it tougher for people to file for bankruptcy and gain a fresh start. Ironically, the industry is also bombarding households with letters urging them to take out credit cards they can't afford and sink further into debt . . . which can lead to bankruptcy. Something doesn't compute—except for the credit card companies' bottom line.

No father wants to be in the position Charles Trapp, a mail carrier in Plantation, Florida, found himself in. In 1992, when his daughter Annelise was four and a half years old, she got sick. At first Trapp and his wife, Lisa, thought that it was nothing more serious than a series of respiratory infections. Then one night, Annelise stopped breathing.

Fortunately, Charles and Lisa were able to resuscitate Annelise. But then, in the hospital, the diagnosis finally came. Annelise had myopathy, a disease similar to a rare form of muscular dystrophy.

She needed a respirator to breathe and a feeding tube to make sure she got enough nutrients.

Soon the family started racking up debt. It wasn't that they lacked health insurance—because both Charles and Lisa were mail carriers, they had a good plan through the United States Postal Service. "But when you have a chronically ill child such as Annelise," Charles Trapp testified to the House Judiciary Committee in February 2001, "even the relatively small portion of her medical expenses that we are responsible for adds up to a considerable amount of debt. Our insurance has paid out literally millions of dollars for Annelise's care. During the worst part of Annelise's illness, we have been forced to use our credit cards for a lot of everyday expenses, such as car repairs, groceries and over-the-counter drugs."

When they had piled up $124,000 in medical bills, $60,000 in credit card debt, still owed $26,000 on their van (purchased so they could take Annelise around town in her wheelchair), not to mention $109,000 on their house, Charles and Lisa had to make a tough decision. They filed for bankruptcy.

AMERICAN FAMILIES ARE MIRED IN CREDIT CARD DEBT
EASIER ACCESS TO CREDIT LINES AND AGRESSIVE MARKETING HAVE PUSHED THE DEBT CARRIED TO NEW HEIGHTS.

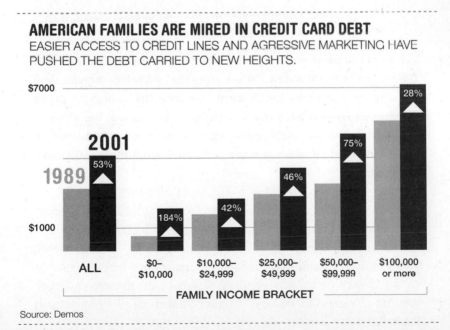

Source: Demos

The Trapps have lots of unfortunate company. Personal bankruptcy rates are on the rise, with 1.7 million in fiscal year 2003, the highest ever. Since 1994, bankruptcy filings in federal courts have increased a whopping 98 percent. Millions more are on the verge of financial disaster, racking up huge amounts of debt. Average credit card debt for an American family rose by 53 percent between 1989 and 2001, from $2,697 to $4,126, according to a recent study by Demos, a New York City think tank. Credit card debt among very low-income families grew by 184 percent, while middle-class families saw an increase of 75 percent. All the while, credit card companies have been counting their profits, which rose 54 percent between 1997 and 2002. Even in hard economic times—or is it because of hard times?—the credit card industry is lucrative.

Contrary to the conventional wisdom, the majority of people who are filing bankruptcy are not frivolous spenders, throwing easy credit card cash at expensive clothes, restaurants, cars, and houses they can't afford. Instead, 9 out of 10 families filing for bankruptcy do so because of job loss, medical problems, divorce, or separation, according to Elizabeth Warren, a professor at Harvard Law School and author, with her daughter, Amelia Warren Tyagi, of *The Two-Income Trap: Why Middle-Class Mothers and Fathers Are Going Broke.*

"The over-consumption myth is just that—a myth," Warren told *Salon.com* in an interview. "It's a story that we tell ourselves. And it's a story that every credit card company that wants to press Congress to give it even more beneficial laws raises: the story of consumers who are wildly spending, and who need to be reined in. The credit card companies need protection from these wild over-spenders."

Warren is referring to bankruptcy reform legislation, backed by the nation's banking and credit card industry, which has been introduced in every congressional session since 1997. Where Warren sees a nation of families trying hard to make ends meet, the credit card industry complains about a nation of deadbeats, and they want to Congress to make it tougher for people to make a fresh start under bankruptcy laws.

Over the years, there have been many versions of this legislation, but at their core are provisions that make it harder for people to qualify to file for bankruptcy under Chapter 7, in which an individual's assets may be liquidated and the proceeds divided among creditors. After this, people are considered free of "unsecured" debt, such as credit card debt, while they are still liable for expenses such as taxes and child support. Credit card companies dislike Chapter 7 because as holders of unsecured

> ★ ★ ★ ★ ★
>
> *"While many members will deny it, the fact is they do not want to cross certain constituencies because it represents too much of the money they need."*
>
> —**Former Representative Tim Penny (D-MN)**, quoted in Speaking Freely, *1st edition, CRP.*

debt, they are last in line to be compensated. The industry prefers that people be forced to file under Chapter 13, which requires people to make a payment plan to pay off all of their debt. They also want to make the rules of Chapter 13 tougher on debtors and more beneficial to the industry and the wealthy. Under its proposals, divorced mothers would find it tougher to collect child support and landlords would find it easier to evict bankrupt tenants. Meanwhile, some rich debtors in five states, where there are "homestead" laws protecting homes during bankruptcy, would be able to keep mansions despite declaring bankruptcy.

The same companies have gone to extraordinary efforts to lure people to spend more on credit than they can afford. Between 1993 and 2000, the industry more than tripled the amount of credit offered to consumers, from $777 billion to almost $3 trillion, according to Demos. The industry has targeted teenagers and college students, and pushed families to pile up the plastic, sending out five billion solicitations through the mail over a one-year period alone, or 50 per U.S. household. "I'm a letter carrier. I see firsthand the incredible number of credit card solicitations mailed out to every one of my customers on my mail route," Charles Trapp told the House Judiciary Committee. "I know how many dozens of mailings Lisa and I personally received over the years."

The big push for bankruptcy reform legislation in Congress is due in no small part to the indefatigable energy of Jeffrey Tassey, first a lobbyist with the American Financial Services Association (AFSA), a trade association representing credit card giants such as MBNA America, General Electric, and Household Financial, and later working for the Washington lobbying firm Williams & Jensen. It was Tassey who, back in 1997, handed a model bill to then-representative Bill McCollum, a Republican from Florida. The lawmaker was no stranger—Tassey had hired one of his former staffers, and he had also held a fundraiser for him. Representative McCollum, who had a seat on the influential Banking and Financial Services Committee, was also the recipient of $374,000 in campaign contributions from the banking and finance/credit industries. In September 1997 McCollum introduced a bill based on the AFSA's recommendations. For

BOUGHT BY CREDIT CARD COMPANIES & BANKS

REPUBLICANS $103.3 million

DEMOCRATS $65.3 million

Source: CRP; includes indiv ($200+), PAC, and soft-money contributions 1989–2004 to federal candidates and parties

doing so, he earned a "Golden Leash" award from Public Campaign, a "symbol of the ties between special interest money and elected officials."

Ever since, the biannual appearance of the bankruptcy bill in every Congressional session has proven an easy line of cash—no need to take out credit—for lobbyists and Members of Congress. The list of K Street mercenaries who have earned money from the bankruptcy bill is a bipartisan Who's Who of the powerful, including Haley Barbour, former Republican National Committee (RNC) chairman; Lloyd Cutler, counsel to Presidents Bill Clinton and Jimmy Carter; and Lloyd Bentsen, former secretary of the treasury under Clinton. The industry has kept the money flowing into politicians' campaign coffers—over $169 million since 1989.

Both the House and the Senate approved bankruptcy reform legislation in 2000, with the support of significant numbers of Democrats, but President Clinton vetoed the bill. In 2002 the legislation went down at the eleventh hour after Senator Chuck

Schumer (D-NY), a staunch opponent, attached a provision that would have prevented anti-abortion protesters from gaining protection in bankruptcy proceedings when they are fined for their protests, forcing conservative senators to vote against the bill. In 2003 the House passed yet another version of bankruptcy reform, by a vote of 315 to 113, including 90 Democrats. "I consider bankruptcy reform to be the equivalent of the Chicago Cubs," lobbyist David P. Goch told the trade journal *Cardline* in October 2003. Despite all the interests lining up behind it, the bankruptcy bill fails to make it into law year after year.

But don't cry for the credit card companies. Back in the 1990s, the financial industry spent year after year and many millions of dollars lobbying for the repeal of Depression-era laws limiting the

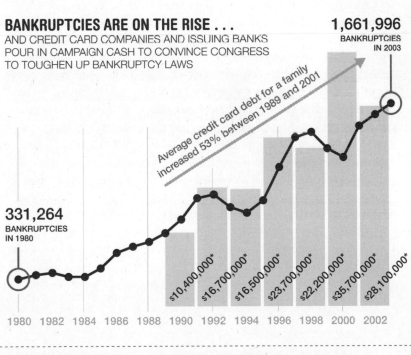

BANKRUPTCIES ARE ON THE RISE . . .

AND CREDIT CARD COMPANIES AND ISSUING BANKS
POUR IN CAMPAIGN CASH TO CONVINCE CONGRESS
TO TOUGHEN UP BANKRUPTCY LAWS

1,661,996
BANKRUPTCIES
IN 2003

Average credit card debt for a family increased 53% between 1989 and 2001

331,264
BANKRUPTCIES
IN 1980

$10,400,000* $16,700,000* $16,500,000* $23,700,000* $22,200,000* $35,700,000* $28,100,000*

1980 1982 1984 1986 1988 1990 1992 1994 1996 1998 2000 2002

Source: American Banking Institute, *CRP; includes indiv ($200+), PAC, and soft-money contributions to federal candidates and parties. Note: Contributions are higher in presidential election years.

ability of banks to get into the securities and insurance business (see chapter 4). The legislation became known around Washington as a gravy train for politicians and lobbyists, and cynical pols noted that it was not necessarily to their disadvantage that the bill always died. After all, they could collect more campaign money and fees when the legislation was introduced again, as it always was. But eventually, Congress approved the bill. While consumer groups have been working hard to oppose the bankruptcy bill in Washington, they are nevertheless ultimately mismatched with the banking and credit card industry on the campaign finance playing field.

Closeup: Charles Cawley

While President Bill Clinton vetoed the bankruptcy reform bill when it landed on his desk, President George W. Bush has indicated he would be much more receptive. Why? Perhaps part of the reason lies with Charles M. Cawley, until recently CEO of credit card giant MBNA Corporation. Cawley, who owns a home in Kennebunkport, Maine, like the president's father, held a fund-raiser there for then-candidate Bush in June 1999, which drew more than 200 attendees. Overall, his company's executives, their families, and its political committee gave the president nearly $240,700 for his 2000 campaign, making MBNA the president's single top contributor, according to the Center for Responsive Politics. Cawley also wrote another $100,000 check to the Bush-Cheney Inaugural Fund.

Needless to say, Cawley earned "Pioneer" status for the 2000 campaign. In the 2004 race, he's aiming to be a "Ranger," pledging to raise at least $200,000. In November 2003, First Lady Laura Bush attended a $2,000-a-person fund-raiser at Cawley's home. "I've known him for a long time," the First Lady told reporters. "This will be a crowd of people who I've known for a long time and been friends with."

Apparently, there are some things that money can just buy. Priceless!

PART SIX

OUR TREASURY IS BEING PLUNDERED

"I believe in the division of labor. You send us to Congress; we pass laws under which you make money . . . and out of your profits, you further contribute to our campaign funds to send us back again to pass more laws to enable you to make more money."

—*Senator Boies Penrose, (R-PA), 1896*

THE RICH GET RICHER . . . AND THE POOR GET AUDITED

While the donor class reaps ever greater tax breaks, and corporations generous to political campaigns pay less and less to Uncle Sam every April, the rest of us are paying a greater share of the taxes. Not only that, poor people are now more likely than the rich to get audited.

How would you like to deduct this as a "business expense" when you do your taxes? Back in 1988, Gary Bielfeldt, a wealthy stockbroker from Peoria, Illinois, used his firm's Learjet to fly in then–house minority leader Bob Michel, former Federal Reserve chairman Paul Volcker, and some investment firm executives to "discuss the markets." Bieldfeldt later testified, "Peoria is not an easy place to get in and out of and if you're going to fly customers in, it's much more convenient for them if you pick them up, fly them in and take them back." He was in court challenging an Internal Revenue Service (IRS) judgment that he owed some $90 million in back taxes.

Amazingly, Bieldfeldt was allowed to deduct most of the $4.9 million he had claimed for the 1988 trip and others using his firm's planes. Over the course of the still unresolved lengthy legal proceedings, for which the court files stand three feet tall, Bieldfeldt hired the best and the brightest to fight the IRS, which has liens on his property worth some $70 million. He now is near settlement with the agency, reports Copley News Service.

To Bill Allison, coauthor of the Center for Public Integrity's book, *The Cheating of America: How Tax Avoidance and Evasion by the Super Rich Are Costing the Country Billions and What You Can Do About It*, the Bielfeldt case is emblematic of how wealthy Americans wriggle out of paying their fair share of taxes even when they face IRS action. "What we found in the book over and over again was wealthy individuals who did have the resources to fight the government and were very adept at it," Allison told the news service.

Yet the facts are even bleaker—wealthy people not only are better positioned to defend themselves against IRS audits than ordinary people, they are also far less likely to get audited in the first place, according to analysis by researchers at Syracuse University. The wealthy are less likely to be audited than they used to be, particularly compared to the poor, and the IRS is getting less tough on corporate tax evaders. Indeed, IRS prosecutions of tax frauds are at an all time low.

Paralleling the IRS action, or inaction, in clamping down on tax fraud is another trend: the wealthy are piling up tax cuts, and, at the same time, corporations are bearing less and less of the nation's tax burden. The effective tax rate for the nation's wealthiest one-

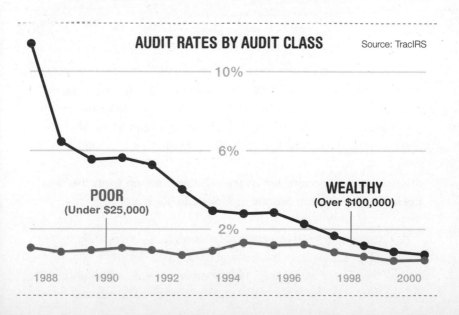

AUDIT RATES BY AUDIT CLASS   Source: TracIRS

10%

6%

POOR
(Under $25,000)

WEALTHY
(Over $100,000)

2%

1988   1990   1992   1994   1996   1998   2000

percent has dropped by 30 percent since 1977, according to Citizens for Tax Justice (CTJ), a Washington watchdog group. Corporate taxes have not been lower since the 1930s, with the exception of one year under President Ronald Reagan. As a share of the economy, corporate taxes here are virtually the lowest in the industrialized world.

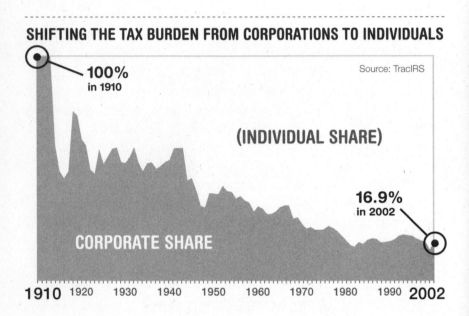

SHIFTING THE TAX BURDEN FROM CORPORATIONS TO INDIVIDUALS

100% in 1910

Source: TracIRS

(INDIVIDUAL SHARE)

16.9% in 2002

CORPORATE SHARE

1910 1920 1930 1940 1950 1960 1970 1980 1990 2002

How did we get in this fix? One clue is that Congress is dependent on campaign contributions from an elite group of givers who are disproportionately wealthy. As the authors of a groundbreaking 1998 academic study of individual congressional campaign contributors (who gave more than $200) wrote,

"Congressional donors are overwhelmingly drawn from the most powerful and affluent groups in American society."

And these donors have a clear agenda when it comes to their own wallets. For example, a solid majority of large donors to congressional candidates wants their taxes cut, "even if it means reducing public services," the 1998 study found. While many business interests lobby for reduced taxes, the fact that most elected officials have to spend the great bulk of their time raising money for their campaigns from this narrow donor class has an additionally invidious effect: even the best-intentioned have a hard time not starting to adopt the world-view of the people they spend so much time with.

Former Democratic senator Bob Kerrey, who was in charge of the Senate Democrats' fund-raising committee in the late 1990s, told journalist Matthew Miller, "I'm not going to ask somebody for money who gets a minimum wage. So I ask somebody who is college educated whose income is over $250,000 a year—and then I have to say things like, 'why don't you get rid of the estate tax, why don't you lower the capital gains tax, why don't you make our tax system less progressive, blah-blah-blah.'"

He who pays the piper calls the tune. President George W. Bush, whose list of volunteer fund-raisers known as "Pioneers" and "Rangers" is riddled with corporate CEOs, has zealously worked to reduce taxes for the wealthy. Tax cuts already enacted by the end of 2003 will cost the Treasury an estimated $209 billion in fiscal year 2005 alone, and a mind-boggling $2.3 trillion dollars through the year 2010 according to CTJ—and that's only if the new tax breaks enacted expire (in his 2004 State of the Union address, the president announced his intention to extend them).

To bring these figures into terms that don't blow gaskets in our brains, that translates into a tax break of about $41,000 in 2005 alone for households averaging $938,000 in income (the wealthiest one percent of Americans), versus $77 for households making an average of $9,800 (the lowest 20 percent of Americans, income-wise.)

All this money has to come from somewhere, and so it's no surprise that massive tax cuts enacted by the Bush Administration are leading to deep cuts in social programs, not to mention an astronomical increase in the national deficit. Under the proposed budget for 2005, seven out of 16 cabinet departments saw budget reductions. These include cuts in the nation's housing program that will lead to at least 250,000 fewer low-income, elderly, and disabled households receiving help, and reductions in grants to states to help out low- and moderate-income working families with day care. Environmental funds to build waste treatment plants and for drinking water facilities are slashed, as is scientific research into troubling environmental issues such as global climate change and the health effects of airborne particulates. Even firefighters, our post-9/11 heroes, face a $250 million cut in grants meant to pay for equipment.

How Corporations Get a Free Ride

It's no wonder that America's corporations are bearing a decreasing share of the national tax burden. Tax shelters have become big business, and mega-corporations are ready and willing to buy. "Squadrons of lawyers, account-ants, and Wall Street structured-finance experts have made an art form of minimizing the U.S. multinational's effective tax rate," Selva Ozelli, interna-tional tax editor for RIA, a New York provider of tax information and software, recently told *Business Week*. A November 2003 Senate Committee investi-gation found that the accounting firm KPMG aggressively marketed tax schemes with enigmatic names like "BLIPS," "FLIPS," "OPIS," and "SC2" to customers looking to escape big tax bites. These arcane shelters earned KPMG $124 million from 350 clients.

These schemes are so complicated that Senator Carl Levin (D-MI), one of the investigators, calls them MEGOs, for "My Eyes Glaze Over." The Gen-eral Accounting Office estimates that these fancy tax shelters could cost the treasury some $85 billion. Some 6,400 individuals and corporations have bought tax shelter "products" from more than 300 firms. Although there are periodic attempts to crack down on tax shelters, the IRS is hobbled by inad-equate budgets, weak enforcement tools, and a meddling Congress all too ready to defend campaign contributors. Here is a (small) sampling of how some companies have used lobby muscle to gain big tax breaks:

- **Foreign Funds.** Tyco International Ltd., Accenture Ltd (formerly an arm of Arthur Andersen), and Ingersoll Rand were among the wave of Ameri-can firms that incorporated overseas in recent years to avoid heftier tax bills here. The move to Bermuda cost Tyco's shareholders $1 billion in capital gains taxes back in 1997, but by 2001, the company was saving some $600 million a year, reports *Business Week*. In 2002, an Ernst & Young tax partner, Kay Barton, told the *New York Times* that incorporat-ing in Bermuda "is a megatrend we are seeing in the marketplace right now." Referring to the post-9/11 era, in a webcast, Barton rhetorically asked her clients,

"Is it the right time to be migrating a corporation's headquarters to an offshore location? . . . [W]e are working with a lot of companies that feel that it is, that just the improvement on earnings is powerful enough that maybe the patriotism issue needs to take a back seat to that."

The closest that Congress has come to closing up the loophole was to vote in 2002 to prevent companies that take advantage of it from securing homeland security contracts, but House Republican leaders excised the provision before it made it into law. (See chapter 24.) Far from becoming pariahs for incorporating overseas, such companies did $1 billion in business with the federal government in 2002, according to an analysis by the Associated Press. AP also reported that these companies had spent $5 million lobbying Congress and federal agencies and donated $1.2 million to campaigns in 2001 and 2002.

- **Me too!** In a flagrant example of me-tooism, Microsoft Corporation lobbied in 1997 to extend a lucrative corporate tax break on export profits to include software. The company's month-by-month campaign contributions that year peaked at $54,100 in July, the same month Congress approved a new law, an 86-word provision tucked into the massive budget reconciliation bill, that extended the tax break to software exporters. Microsoft won't say exactly how much it has saved from the tax break. Meanwhile, Boeing Company, General Electric, Monsanto, RJR Nabisco, and a half dozen other companies saved some $2.6 billion between 1991 and 1998 on the same tax break, which has since been declared an illegal subsidy by the World Trade Organization. The companies contributed a total of $34 million to political campaigns and party committees between 1991 and 2000.

- **No taxes at all.** Corporate America has long lusted to eliminate the corporate alternative minimum tax (AMT), which ensures that profitable companies not abuse the tax code to avoid paying any taxes. Under the economic stimulus bill narrowly passed by the Republican-controlled House after 9/11, which was loaded down with $212 billion in tax cuts, not only was the AMT repealed, all the payments made under it since 1986 were to be rebated. Just 16 profitable companies, including household names such as ChevronTexaco, IBM, General Electric, and General Motors, stood to gain $7.4 billion in immediate tax rebates. These same companies were the source of nearly $46 million in campaign contributions to federal candidates and party committees from 1991 through 2002, two-thirds of that to the GOP, including half a million dollars for President George Bush's 2000 campaign. Public outrage at the brazenness of that money grab ultimately forced Congress to shelve its efforts to repeal the AMT—especially after the press started reporting that Enron, the high-flying and troubled energy company with close ties to the Bush administration, would get an immediate tax rebate check of $254 million.

Kenneth Kies, Uber–Tax Lobbyist

Come April 15, when you are despairing over piles of receipts, pages of technical Internal Revenue Service (IRS) instructions, and wondering if it's too late to get an extension on your tax filing, what if you could call in the likes of Kenneth Kies to help you out?

"Who is Kenneth Kies?" you ask. He's hardly a household name, like Donald Trump or Warren Buffett. But if you were a corporate CEO you would certainly know who Kies is. As one of the nation's most powerful tax lobbyists, he's saved corporations millions of dollars in taxes by preserving arcane tax breaks. His clients have included Bank of America, General Electric, Goldman Sachs & Co., General Motors, and IBM, all major campaign contributors.

To understand how Kies earns his livelihood, consider the example of synthetic coal. Back in the 1970s, during the energy crisis, Congress created a tax break designed to encourage industry to turn coal into synthetic fuel as a means to reduce dependence on foreign oil. The synthetic fuel industry never caught on, though, until 20 years later, when clever tax lawyers figured out a way to use it to save money for clients. To qualify for the tax break, you see, makers of synthetic fuel need only prove that they have modified the chemical composition of coal. There is no requirement that the resulting fuel be less polluting, or better than other fuels, nothing.

Soon companies that were never in the energy business, like the hotel chain Marriott International Inc., jumped into the synthetic fuel game. According to *Time* magazine's Donald L. Barlett and James B. Steele, Marriott bought four synfuel plants in October 2001, and by the next year was generating $159 million in tax credits. The company's 2002 annual report boasted that its effective tax rate plummeted to 6.8% from 36.1% in 2001, "primarily due to the impact of our synthetic-fuel business." Barlett and Steele estimate that the synfuel tax credit costs the Treasury some $1 billion annually.

In 2003 the IRS decided to investigate the synfuel tax credits. Needless to say, those enjoying synfuel tax credits were not pleased.

Enter Kenneth Kies. Kies represented a group of companies called the "Council for Energy Independence" (vaguely named coalitions are a staple of the Washington lobbying world), whose members included synfuel developers, owners, and users such as GE Capital Services, Koch Industries, and Teco Energy. Kies, who had admitted to Barlett and Steele that "People only do [synthetic fuel] because of the tax credit," got to work, arranging meetings with members of Congress and IRS officials. "There is a lot of energy being put forth on behalf of taxpayers to force the IRS to back off of this," he told the magazine. Soon members of Congress from coal-states, such as Senators Richard Shelby (R-AL), Jim Bunning (R-KY), and John Rockefeller (D-WV) were protesting the IRS's actions.

The IRS backed off. In October 2003 the agency said that that the synthetic fuel created from coal is "scientifically valid," and that it would start issuing approval letters again to companies seeking synthetic-fuel tax credits. Kies told the *Washington Post* the announcement allowed "the industry to get back to business as usual."

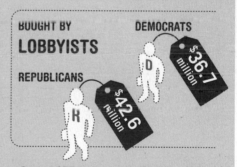

Source: CRP; includes indiv ($200+), PAC, and soft-money contributions 1989–2004 to federal candidates and parties

How does Kies do it? Consider his résumé. Kies has gone through the revolving door between government service and private lobbying twice. Between 1981 and 1986, he served on the Republican staff of the House Ways and Means Committee, "Tax-Writing Central," rising to position of chief minority tax counsel and working on several key Reagan-era tax bills before leaving for the Washington, D.C., office of Baker & Hostetler, where he earned $600,000 a year.

Then came the elections of 1994 and the Republican takeover of

Congress. The morning after the elections, on November 2, 1994, Kies got a phone call from Representative Bill Archer (R-TX). Archer wanted Kies to become chief of staff of the Joint Committee on Taxation. Kies jumped at the chance, even though it meant a pay cut of nearly half a million dollars.

Four years later, when Kies decided to leave Capitol Hill again, there was a bidding war. Kies was "recruited by lobby shops the way college basketball coaches go after a 7-footer with a jump shot," the newspaper *Legal Times* put it. The accounting firm PricewaterhouseCoopers won the contest, landing Kies at a reported $1 million annual salary. After the Enron scandal, PricewaterhouseCoopers jettisoned its lobbying business, and Kies is now at the firm Clark/Bardes, working with several other House Ways and Means alumni.

Kies relies on his expertise, his relationships from jobs past, and of course, campaign contributions, to deliver to his corporate clients. He and his wife, Kathleen, also a lobbyist, have personally contributed more than $331,000 since 1989 to federal candidates and parties, 96 percent of that to Republicans. Kies also helps raise campaign contributions from others. Amounts are difficult to track, since this sort of activity is not reported to the Federal Election Commission. However, Kies was one of a group of lobbyists who were wooed by the Bush campaign at a barbecue in Crawford, Texas, in August 2003, where attendees got to shmooze with Karl Rove and Mercer Reynolds III, the campaign's finance chairman, among other Bush team star strategists, and were encouraged to become Bush "Pioneers."

LOBBYISTS AND THE 2004 PRESIDENTIAL CANDIDATES

Source: CRP; includes indiv ($200+) and PAC contributions

$981,726.....GEORGE W BUSH (R)
$236,974...RICHARD A GEPHARDT (D)
$235,050...JOHN KERRY (D)
$118,435...JOE LIEBERMAN (D)
$67,250...BOB GRAHAM (D)
$60,168...HOWARD DEAN (D)
$47,650...WESLEY CLARK (D)
$22,380...JOHN EDWARDS (D)
$6,750....CAROL MOSELEY BRAUN (D)
$1,000...AL SHARPTON (D)

In February 2001 Kies was one of the lobbyists tapped to help Representative Bill Thomas (R-CA), then new chairman of the House Ways and Means Committee, raise $6 million for House Republicans, according to a report in the *Wall Street Journal.* He also helped raise funds for a GOP fundraiser in June 2000 that netted $9 million, according to the Associated Press.

While Kies may represent the crème-de-la-crème of lobbyists, he is just a high-ranking officer in the army that has sacked the nation's capitol. As a group, lobbyists have contributed more than $79.3 million to federal campaigns since 1989.

CORPORATE WELFARE, LAND-GRAB STYLE

Nearly one-third of the United States is public land. That means we, the taxpayers, own it. But we don't get fair value for its use when the mining, grazing, and timber industries extract resources from our land. Instead we get fleeced. The reason: The millions of dollars in campaign contributions that politicians have collected from these industries over the years. And now land-grab lobbyists are running the government agencies that they used to lobby!

As taxpayers we are real estate rich, owning some 652 million acres of public land, nearly one-third of the entire landmass of the United States. The powerful geysers of Yellowstone, the reds and oranges of the deep sedimentary layers of the Grand Canyon, the wildflower-strewn meadows of the Sierras, all are part of this great commonwealth. However, only a small proportion of this land is protected in national parks. On the rest of it, the mining, grazing, and timber industries are reaping huge profits by extracting resources, while not paying taxpayers what these resources are worth.

Archaic Mining Law

The year is 1872. Congress eliminates the income tax enacted during the Civil War. Louis Pasteur proves that microorganisms cause fermentation. Anthony Comstock pushes for a law to prohibit the transport of contraceptives. Susan B. Anthony and other suffragettes get arrested for trying to vote in the presidential election, which Ulysses Grant wins. And President Grant approves the General Mining law, still the law of our land more than 130 years later.

Designed to encourage development in the then–Wild West, the 1872 mining law allows anybody to file a hard-rock mining claim on large swathes of public land simply by driving four stakes into the ground to mark a 20-acre tract and paying $100. If you are lucky enough to strike gold, or silver, or uranium, or whatever metal you are looking for, then you can extract it, process it, and sell it without paying any royalty payment whatsoever to compensate taxpayers, unlike industries mining for coal, oil, and gas on public lands. More than a century later, the law is still on the books and the U.S. Treasury is getting fleeced, big-time. According to the watchdog group Taxpayers for Common Sense, the 1872 mining law cost taxpayers some $100 million in 2000 alone.

What's more, taxpayers are all too often liable for the mess that mining companies leave behind. More than half a million abandoned mines dot the mountains and valleys largely in the west, and they have left a legacy of pollution. At least 40 percent of the headwaters of western watersheds are contaminated, according to the Environmental Protection Agency, and cleanup costs are estimated at anywhere from $32 billion to $72 billion.

BOUGHT BY   DEMOCRATS

THE MINING INDUSTRY

REPUBLICANS

D $6 million

R $20.4 million

Source: CRP; includes indiv ($200+), PAC, and soft-money contributions 1989–2004 to federal candidates and parties

Many of these sites are now on the nation's Superfund list for areas needing toxic cleanup, which the taxpayers bear the brunt for paying. (See chapter 13.)

This sweetheart deal just gets sweeter. The law also contains a provision that allows people with mining claims to buy the land from the government for the 1872 price of $5 an acre or less, if they show that there are enough minerals in there to make it profitable to mine. Since 1867, the federal government has sold off some 3.3 million acres of public land under this "patenting" program, an area larger than the state of Connecticut. For example, in 1994, the Canadian-based Barrick Resources secured more than 1,800 acres for an estimated price of $9,000. The estimated worth of the gold on this land was more than $10 billion. (Once the land is purchased, however, the owner is not obliged to mine the land, and, indeed, there are cases where people have instead used the land for real estate developments, casinos, and golf courses.) These sorts of outrageous giveaways prompted Congress, in 1994, to establish a year-long moratorium on new patents, which has been renewed each year since; however, hundreds of patents were grandfathered in at the time, and the moratorium is vulnerable since it expires annually.

Thanks to effective lobbying by the mining industry, which has contributed $26.7 million to federal campaigns since 1989, and the support companies find in western lawmakers, those in Congress who have tried to reform the 1872 mining law have yet to succeed. Former senator Dale Bumpers (D-AR) spent nine years trying before retiring in 1998.

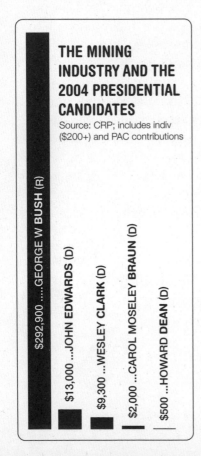

THE MINING INDUSTRY AND THE 2004 PRESIDENTIAL CANDIDATES

Source: CRP; includes indiv ($200+) and PAC contributions

$292,900 ..... GEORGE W BUSH (R)

$13,000 ... JOHN EDWARDS (D)

$9,300 ... WESLEY CLARK (D)

$2,000 ... CAROL MOSELEY BRAUN (D)

$500 ... HOWARD DEAN (D)

"It seems incomprehensible that Congress would allow this abuse of taxpayers to continue," he wrote in the *Washington Monthly* that year. "How could this be? Well, as my mother used to say, 'Everybody's business is nobody's business.'"

Bumpers added, "And the unpleasant truth is that it is much more important to the mining industry and members of Congress from mining states to maintain the status quo than it is for the public, largely unaware that it is being used and abused, to demand and achieve change." Bumpers' heir in mining reform is Representative Nick Rahall (D-WV), who introduced a comprehensive mining reform bill supported by environmental and taxpayer groups in May 2003. The legislation has yet to receive even a hearing in committee.

Who's in Charge: Steven Griles

"Time to party!" yelled a lobbyist on his way to the $3,000-per-corporation "Mulligans and Margaritas" golf fundraiser in Arizona in January 2004 benefiting Western Republican congressional campaigns. The bash was held in conjunction with a three-day energy industry conference where Steven Griles, deputy interior secrotary, was a luncheon speaker. Before he became a bureaucrat, Griles was a lobbyist for the mining industry; his clients included the National Mining Association and a host of coal companies. Even as he pulls a government paycheck, Griles is receiving more than half a million dollars over two years from his former lobbying firm, National Environmental Strategies, "in recognition of the client base" he built at the firm. As an Interior official, he's pushed to make it easier for companies to mine coal by using a technique called "mountain top removal," in which they literally blast the tops off mountains and dump the waste into streams. In October 2001 he wrote a memo to top agency officials, criticizing a draft environmental impact statement that concluded that vast portions of the Appalachian environment would be destroyed if mountaintop removal continued unchecked. Just one month after the memo was sent, coal interests contributed $150,350 in soft money to the Republican National Committee.

Grazing on Taxpayer Money

Anyone who has traveled on a country road in the West is used to the sight of a herd of cattle crossing the road. (The trick is to blast your horn and drive right on through.) If those cattle are grazing on public lands, they do so at a significant discount to the rancher and a great cost to the taxpayer. While ranchers pay anywhere from $7 (in Arizona) to $20 (in Nebraska) for the amount of forage it takes to feed a cow grazing for a month on private land, when their cattle grazes on Uncle Sam's land the cost is just $1.43.

The amount the government collects from these discount fees does not even begin to pay for the costs of the program, estimated at between $500 million and $1 billion annually in a study commissioned by the Center for Biological Diversity and conducted by a U.S. Bureau of Land Management economist and a University of Kentucky professor. That estimate includes the direct cost of administering the program but also other expenses you might not think of immediately, such as killing bobcats, black bears, coyotes, and other predators that might attack the cattle and controlling flooding on over-grazed land, all services provided by the U.S. government (and therefore you, the taxpayer). The formidable ranching lobby has been successful in driving off attempts to reform the grazing system, herding lawmakers with campaign cash. Cattlemen have contributed $22.6 million to federal campaigns since 1989.

In the early 1990s, then–interior secretary Bruce Babbitt vowed to reform the grazing fees program. However, a group of western senators, led by Senator Pete Domenici (R-NM) and Senator Max Baucus (D-MT)—the number 6 and number 15 top recipients for lifetime Senate campaign contributions from livestock interests, respectively—successfully filibustered against the proposal. Under more pressure, Babbitt later backed off plans to raise the fees through reg-

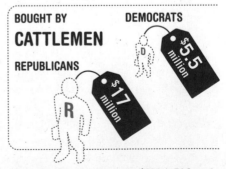

BOUGHT BY **DEMOCRATS**

CATTLEMEN

REPUBLICANS

$5.5 million

$17 million

Source: CRP; includes indiv ($200+), PAC, and soft-money contributions 1989–2004 to federal candidates and parties

ulations. Other attempts since in Congress to raise the fees have all failed.

In December 2003 the Bush administration's Interior Department proposed new regulations that made ranchers happy, but environmentalists fume. The new rules not only do nothing about raising grazing fees, they also roll back environmental protections established in the Babbitt years. "We're very pleased," remarked Bill Higgins, executive vice president of the California Cattlemen's Association to the *Fresno Bee*. "They took the industry's input into

Who's in Charge: William Myers

THE LIVESTOCK INDUSTRY AND THE 2004 PRESIDENTIAL CANDIDATES

Source: CRP; includes indiv ($200+) and PAC contributions

$449,300 ..... GEORGE W BUSH (R)

$13,000...WESLEY CLARK (D)

$8,300...JOHN EDWARDS (D)

$8,200...JOHN KERRY (D)

$6,000...HOWARD DEAN (D)

$4,500...RICHARD A GEPHARDT (D)

$1,000...JOE LIEBERMAN (D)

$750...BOB GRAHAM (D)

$500...DENNIS J KUCINICH (D)

Until President George W. Bush tapped him as his nominee for the Ninth Circuit Court of Appeals, William Myers was his solicitor at the Department of Interior. Before that, he worked in Idaho as an attorney for the firm Holland & Hart, and he served as a lobbyist for pro-grazing trade associations such as the National Cattlemen's Beef Association, the Association of National Grasslands, and the American Sheep Industry Association. While at the Interior Department, he met at least 27 times with individuals and groups with an interest in grazing and mining policies, and he wrote a legal opinion questioning the agency's plan to retire grazing permits at Utah's Grand Staircase-Escalante National Monument. He also presided over the rolling back of Bruce Babbitt's grazing regulations.

consideration, and we're hopeful that these rules at the end of the day will provide for greater management flexibility."

How the Timber Crowd Shouts "Fire" in the Forests

The past several years, as drought has plagued the western states, the end of winter means the beginning of wildfire season. Since 2002 alone the Forest Service has fought fires on some 11 million acres, from the forests east of Los Angeles to the Rocky Mountains of Colorado to the lush forests of the Northwest. This might seem right and

natural for the government agency to do—after all, didn't we grow up with Smokey the Bear, who hated forest fires? And haven't we all seen reports of people being evacuated from their homes, as smoke clogs the sky and fire licks at their lawns?

Environmental thinking, however, has changed since the original "Smokey" was pulled out of a New Mexico fire in 1950. Experts now say that fires are as natural to forests as sun is to desert, or snow is to high mountains—that they are part of the natural balance of the ecosystem. Indeed, years of eager firefighting has contributed to the current spate of fierce fires, because past fire-suppression efforts have left behind flammable material that burns faster and hotter. And while many homes have been destroyed and threatened in western fires—a trend exacerbated as real estate developers push further into the wilderness—this threat can be mitigated when homeowners take simple steps, such as thinning trees near their houses and refraining from using flammable shake shingles on their roofs. Indeed, many localities

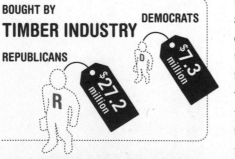

BOUGHT BY
TIMBER INDUSTRY
REPUBLICANS
DEMOCRATS
R $27.2 million
D $7.3 million

Source: CRP; includes indiv ($200+), PAC, and soft-money contributions 1989–2004 to federal candidates and parties

in threatened areas are now approving building codes that require just these things.

The fact is, wildfire fighting has become big business—for the Forest Service, and other agencies that combat them, that is. After the 2000 fire season, when more than eight million acres burned, Congress nearly doubled the federal firefighting budget from $1.6 billion to $2.9 billion, all taxpayer money, of course. For the Forest Service, which had been facing shrinking budgets as timber

Who's In Charge: Mark Rey

Former timber lobbyist Mark Rey was the Bush administration's choice for the position of managing the nation's 191 million acres of national forests in 44 states. Rey, who is undersecretary of natural resources and environment for the U.S. Department of Agriculture (the Forest Service is a sub-agency of USDA) spent nearly 20 years working for a number of timber trade associations, including the American Paper Institute, the National Forest Products Association, and the American Forest Resources Alliance. Rey made a name for himself in the early 1990s fighting against legislative efforts to protect old growth forests in the Northwest. With the Republican takeover of Congress, Rey became a staff member on the Senate Committee on Energy and Natural Resources, where he was the architect in 1995 of the "salvage rider," which accelerated clear-cutting in old-growth forests.

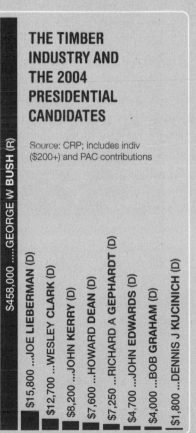

THE TIMBER INDUSTRY AND THE 2004 PRESIDENTIAL CANDIDATES

Source: CRP; includes indiv ($200+) and PAC contributions

$458,000 .....GEORGE W BUSH (R)
$15,800 ...JOE LIEBERMAN (D)
$12,700 ...WESLEY CLARK (D)
$8,200 ...JOHN KERRY (D)
$7,600 ...HOWARD DEAN (D)
$7,250 ...RICHARD A GEPHARDT (D)
$4,700 ...JOHN EDWARDS (D)
$4,000 ...BOB GRAHAM (D)
$1,800 ...DENNIS J KUCINICH (D)

sales on public lands have declined following years of successful protests by environmental groups, the wildfires also have meant a chance to reconnect with an old friend: the timber industry. Since 1989, the timber industry has contributed $34.5 million to federal campaigns.

In December 2003, when President George W. Bush signed the new "Healthy Forests Restoration" law, he said, "We have a responsibility to be good stewards of our forests. That's a solemn responsibility. . . . With the Healthy Forest Restoration Act, we will help to prevent catastrophic wildfires. We'll help save lives and property. And we'll help protect our forests from sudden and needless destruction."

But environmentalists call the legislation, which Congress had debated during the height of the wildfire season, a giveaway to the timber industry because it would make it easier for companies to log deep in the forests. The law concentrates on "fuel reduction," thinning combustible materials in the forest to prevent forest fires, much of which will be done by, yes, the timber industry, mostly nowhere near threatened communities, which may indeed need such help, but rather deep in to the forest, where valuable timber is. The new law severely limits the ability of the public to file appeals and ask for reviews of timber sales, long a bugaboo for the timber industry.

Adding insult to injury for taxpayers, the Forest Service never had the reputation for managing timber sales well. In 1998, the last year for which an estimate is available (thanks to poor data reporting by the Forest Service), the Forest Service's timber sale program cost $407 million, according to analysis by Taxpayers for Common Sense. Previously, the General Accounting Office estimated that the Forest Service timber program cost more than $2 billion between 1992 and 1997. One reason why: there is so little competition for the lumber. Nearly one-third of timber sales are sold with only one bid, according to analysis by the taxpayer watchdog group, and 70 percent of sales had no more than two bids. The Forest Service consistently charges less for timber than it costs to prepare it for sale.

THE FARMER IN
THE TILL

Taxpayers spend billions of dollars on subsidies to agribusiness— and we get back higher prices, more pollution, and fewer choices at the supermarket. All this thanks to the tremendous influence of agribusiness in Washington, which fertilizes political campaigns with millions of dollars, particularly to those politicians who are members of the House and Senate Agriculture Committees. Talk about "pigging out"!

The John Hancock Mutual Life Insurance company opened its doors in 1862 in downtown Boston, starting as a one-room, four-person operation selling life insurance. Since then, the company has grown into a financial services giant, selling not just life insurance, but also mutual funds and long-term care insurance coverage.

John Hancock is also one of the nation's top recipients of peanut subsidies. Yes, peanut subsidies. In 2002, the company collected more than $2 million from taxpayers as part of a new "buy out" program tucked into farm legislation approved by Congress earlier that year.

Admittedly, $2 million is peanuts for a company with $8.5 billion in revenues in 2002. But it's emblematic of the crazy nature of taxpayer-funded agriculture subsidies, in which the hog's share of funding flows to the largest farms, and sometimes even to corporations, such as Chevron, Westvaco, and Dupont, whose CEOs likely never go near a peanut or wheat or cotton field.

Between 1995 and 2002, taxpayers seeded agribusiness with $114 billion in subsidies, according to the Environmental Working Group. Eight in ten of those dollars went to boost the income of crop farmers, and to a lesser extent, livestock farmers. Another 12.5 percent went to conservation programs meant to encourage farmers to preserve the environment. Over this time period, the conservation funding declined while the funding for commodity crops increased considerably. Meanwhile, more than two-thirds of agriculture payments went to the top ten percent of subsidy recipients, a trend that worsened as the years went by.

The agriculture subsidy system has contributed to the growth of agribusiness and the decline of family farming, by encouraging large operations over small ones. Since the mid-1930s, the number of farms in America has decreased from nearly 7 million to about 2 million today, even as the acreage size of farms has increased from less than 200 acres to nearly 500 acres.

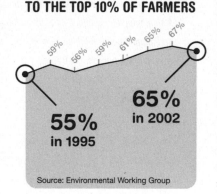

AGRICULTURAL PAYMENTS GOING TO THE TOP 10% OF FARMERS

59% 56% 59% 61% 65% 67%

55% in 1995

65% in 2002

Source: Environmental Working Group

The concentration of farming in fewer hands doesn't stop with wheat, corn, and soybeans. Cows, hogs, poultry, and other livestock increasingly are crowded into corporate-owned factory farms, which produce enormous piles of animal waste, some 2.7 trillion pounds per year. The waste seeps into rivers and streams, killing fish and polluting drinking water. A handful of agricultural conglomerates, such as ConAgra and Cargill, control these factory farms by commanding most aspects of meat production. These mammoth companies sell the feed for the animals, contract to purchase them from the farmers, and then process and sell the meat, all according to their own specifications. Small livestock farmers have a tough time competing, because there just isn't much of a market for them to sell their meat.

How has farming gotten into such a fix in this country, where bigger is better and family farms have become an endangered species? Much of the answer can be found in the nation's capital, where, every five years or so, Congress engages in the ritual of writing a new farm bill, which governs agriculture policy for the nation. Agribusiness is

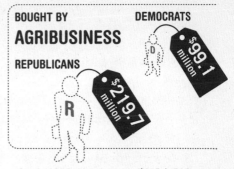

Source: CRP; includes indiv ($200+), PAC, and soft-money contributions 1989–2004 to federal candidates and parties

generous to politicians, and has contributed $319.5 million to federal political campaigns since 1989.

When debate on the most recent farm bill was heating up in the Senate, there was more pressure than ever from family farm groups and environmentalists to limit subsidy payments to farmers, open up the livestock market, and strengthen environmental protections. Fiscal conservatives also lined up to oppose farm subsidies. A survey of rural Nebraskans by the University of Nebraska–Lincoln in the summer showed that 73 percent of respondents supported the idea of limiting payments to farmers.

"It's our position that a farmer can farm as much land as he wants, but there comes a time there ought to be a limit on the amount of money the government gives him, so we don't have farmers living off the government, and putting other farmers out of business," Gary Hoskey, president of the Iowa Farmers Union, told the Iowa Waterloo Courier.

In December 2001 the Senate actually voted, in a squeaker, 51 to 46, to make it unlawful for a meatpacker to own, feed, or control livestock intended for slaughter. A few months later, in February, in a voice vote, the Senate capped subsidy payments to farmers at $275,000. But the House had included a much higher subsidy limit, of $550,000, in its version of the bill, and there was no ban on meatpackers owning livestock.

When the House and Senate approve different versions of legislation, it's up to a conference committee made up of members from both bodies to reconcile the differences. When the farm bill committee finished its deliberations, the subsidy limits were gutted. While there was still a new limit of $360,000 per farmer, there were enough loopholes attached such that the limit no longer meant much. And the ban on livestock owned by meatpackers was gone. The 14 core House members of this conference committee, all of whom were members of the House Agriculture Committee, collected an average of $33,144 from agribusiness interests toward the 2002 election, while the seven Senate members averaged $142,518 over a six-year Senate cycle. The farm bill that became law increased federal payments to farmers by at least $83 billion over 10 years. (In a nice post-9/11 touch, it was renamed the Farm Security bill, as if big handouts to fatcat farmers was somehow enhancing national security.)

> ★ ★ ★ ★ ★
>
> *"Money creates the relationships. Companies with interests before particular committees need to have access to the chairman of that committee, make donations, and go to events where the chairman will be. Even if that chairman is not the type of Member who will tie the contribution and the legislative goals together, donors can't be sure so they want to play it safe."*
>
> —*Robert Rozen, lobbyist with Washington Council Ernst & Young,* declaration for McConnell v. FEC

Now back to peanuts and John Hancock Mutual Life Insurance Company. Also tucked in the new farm bill was a "buy-out" program for peanut quotas. The federal peanut program, dating back to the Depression, ran on a complicated quota system, in which farmers who wanted to grow or sell peanuts were required to own "quotas." They were allowed to lease the quotas to others, however, and a majority of them did, to people or companies that bought them for investment purchases. Under the 2002 farm bill, taxpayers are obliged to give peanut quota holders cash payments to pay for their exclusive license to sell peanuts at an artificially high price.

Peanut growers also got a commodity support program of their own, similar to that of other crops. Which is why you, the taxpayer, paid more than $2 million to John Hancock Mutual Life Insurance Company, part of $1.1 billion paid out to peanut quota owners in 2002.

It may be a bit rash to condemn the insurance company, however, for having no interest in peanuts whatsoever. A few years ago, the company became a sponsor of the John Hancock All-Star Fan-Fest for Major League Baseball. At a fanfest in 2002 in Seattle, a public relations firm hired by the company orchestrated "peanut-shelling' events around town, featuring local celebrity Rick 'The Peanut Man' Kaminski. Insurance . . . baseball . . . peanut subsidies—perhaps they are all as American as apple pie. (And yes, the farm bill also added new subsidies for apple growers.)

Sweet Subsidies

For Washington power watchers, one of the most titillating pieces of information contained in the 445-page Clinton impeachment report released by Kenneth Starr in 1998 was not the tales of trysts between the president and the intern, but rather who called during those encounters. On February 19, 1996, according to the Starr report, Lewinsky recalled

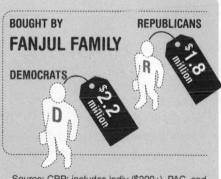

Source: CRP; includes indiv ($200+), PAC, and soft-money contributions 1989–2004 to federal candidates and parties

that while the president was telling her he thought their intimate relationship should end, he received a call from "a sugar grower in Florida whose name . . . was something like 'Fanuli.'" When the Starr team checked the president's phone log, they found that he had talked with Alfonso Fanjul of Palm Beach, Florida, that day for about 20 minutes.

That the Fanjul family of Florida was the first family of sugar, with tremendous political pull on both sides of the party aisle, was already well known in Washington. Over the years, the family, its companies and their employees have contributed more than $4.0 million since 1989 to federal candidates, parties, and leadership PACs.

Alfie Fanjul was Bill Clinton's Florida campaign co-chairman in 1992. His brother, Jose "Pepe" Fanjul, the Republican in the family, had been the national vice chairman of finance for Bob Dole's presidential campaign in 1996. But the Lewinsky recollection clinched it—here was a family of generous donors who had direct access to the president, even in the midst of an illicit rendezvous.

The Fanjul family has carefully cultivated politicians along with its 180,000 acres of sugar cane in the Florida Everglades for obvious reasons. The Depression-era sugar program in this country guarantees the price of sugar for sugar cane and beet growers and limits imports. The result is higher prices for consumers—about 50 cents more for a five-pound bag of sugar —and millions of dollars for sugar growers. For the Fanjul family, one of the two largest sugar growers in Florida, this translates into approximately $65 million a year in benefits, according to a General Accounting Office analysis.

And that doesn't even count all the other benefits they reap from the U.S. government. The U.S. government also assigns quotas to 40 countries for the sugar that domestic producers cannot provide. The Dominican Republic is the largest quota holder, and yes, the Fanjuls grow sugar there, too.

In the national arena, the sugar industry has beat back numerous attempts to reform the sugar program. Before he retired in 2002, Florida Representative Dan Miller (R-FL) tried and failed four times to eliminate the subsidy. He is not the only one who has made an attempt. In the 2002 farm bill debate, the Senate voted against an amendment, 71 to 29, by Senator Judd Gregg (R-NH) to eliminate the federal sugar program and use the savings to boost the food-stamp program. Senators who voted in favor of the the sugar industry's position received 24 times as much campaign cash from sugar growers as those who didn't.

Meanwhile, the Fanjul family is continuing to share sweet talk with whoever is in the highest office in the country. Pepe Fanjul has become a Bush "Ranger," promising to raise at least $200,000 for the president's 2004 reelection campaign.

HOMELAND SECURITY OR PROFIT SECURITY?

The nation mourned and many suffered. But while we had our hands over our hearts, saluting the sacrifice of the many who died on September 11, 2001, wealthy special interests like the airline industry, the pharmaceutical industry, and the insurance industry swarmed over Capitol Hill, picking our pockets.

Eleven days after the terrorist attacks of September 11, Congress rushed through a $15 billion bailout of the airline industry—$5 billion in cash and the rest in loan guarantees. It did nothing to address the needs of more than 140,000 airline workers whose jobs were imperiled by the attacks. The larger travel and tourism sector got no relief from Congress either, even though it employed two million people at the time. The travel industry estimated losing $1.36 billion in the four weeks after the terror attacks of September 11.

With airline travel shut down after attacks, few could assail the decision to compensate the airline companies for the losses they suffered. That said, the questions have only multiplied about how Congress set its priorities in addressing the crisis. These questions are worth asking still, as many towns and cities across the country complain that they don't have the money to pay for expanded homeland security functions.

As former Republican senator Warren Rudman concluded in a

2003 report for the Council on Foreign Relations, "The United States is drastically underfunding local emergency responders and remains dangerously unprepared to handle a catastrophic attack on American soil." He added, "If you talk to mayors, to governors, to police chiefs, they are just not ready, and we had better get ready." According to the

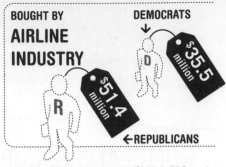

Source: CRP; includes indiv ($200+), PAC, and soft-money contributions 1989–2004 to federal candidates and parties

National Fire Protection Association, only 11 percent of departments around the country have the people and equipment needed to respond to a serious building collapse. Only 13 percent are prepared for an incident involving chemical or biological agents and at least 10 injuries. Most police, fire, and other public safety agencies don't even have mutually compatible communications systems, which hurt rescue efforts at the World Trade Center.

The Council on Foreign Relations report called for a fivefold increase in federal funding for federal, state and local first-responders, from $5 billion to $25 billion a year. But actual funding levels are falling far short. For example, since 9/11, the government has only provided about $500 million to local authorities to enhance port security. The U.S. Coast Guard says they will need a little more than ten times that figure to comply with new federal security regulations. In the meantime, only one to two percent of the nearly six million cargo containers entering the country annually are inspected. President Bush's budget request for the 2005 fiscal year provides just $46 million to meet port facility security requirements. The Association of American Port Authorities called this funding gap "disheartening."

Why are some narrow interests in profit security being served, while the broader public interest in homeland security goes begging? Alas, the answer comes back to big money in politics.

One vocal critic of the 2001 airline bailout was Senator Peter Fitzgerald, a Republican from Illinois who was the sole senator to vote against it. He told a group of travel industry executives and labor leaders who came to Congress that fall to seek aid:

"Other industries don't have the raw political clout the airlines have. . . . The payouts to the airline industry were grossly excessive," Fitzgerald added. "The only people who got bailed out were the shareholders. The one million airline employees were left twisting in the wind."

How did the airlines get to the head of the bailout line? And how did they end up getting more money out of taxpayers than they lost in the three days the nation's airports were shut down? By moving fast and without shame to deploy a crack army of lobbyists on Capitol Hill and by using all the access and influence that could be bought with $65.8 million in campaign contributions over the previous eleven years. (The industry has continued to curry favor in Washington since the beginning of 2001, airlifting in another $21.2 million in cash.)

The airlines had plenty of well-placed helpers in their quest for the bailout. According to a report by Public Citizen, current or recent airline lobbyists include Linda Hall Daschle (wife of Senate majority leader Tom Daschle (D-SD), the number 5 lifetime recipient of air industry cash in the Senate at $252,350); Haley Barbour (former Republican National Committee chair), Harold Ickes (former Clinton deputy chief of staff), Ken Duberstein (former Reagan chief of staff and a crony of Colin Powell), Nick Calio (then President Bush's congressional liaison), and former senators Dale Bumpers (D-AR) and Bob Packwood (R-OR).

The airline lobby went to work right away, on September 12. "It was masterful," said Senator Fitzgerald to the *New York Times*. "The airline

> ⋆ ⋆ ⋆ ⋆ ⋆
>
> *"What happened was a tragedy, certainly, but there are opportunities. We're in business. This is not a charity."*
>
> —*James Albertine, president of the American League of Lobbyists, explaining the rush by Washington lobbyists after 9/11 to repackage their positions as patriotic responses to the attacks. Source: the* New York Times, *December 3, 2001.*

industry made a full-court press to convince Congress that giving them billions in taxpayer cash was the only way to save the republic." Representative George Miller (D-CA) remarked,

"The big dog got the bone. After Sept. 11, the mood was one of shared sacrifice. People had lost their jobs and their lives. And the first thing that happened was the airline industry came in while everyone else is waiting to see if they can make their mortgage payments."

Critics have also noted that there was no way to tell how much of the airline bailout would also go to prop up heavily indebted airlines like US Airways, America West, and Northwest, which were tottering toward bankruptcy well before September 11. And unlike the government bailout of Chrysler two decades ago, the airlines' stakeholders were not asked to make any concessions. Banks did not have to forgive or stretch out any airline debts, for example. Nor did airline executives have to take a cut in pay.

Not only that, the airlines, airports and airline security firms involved in the 9/11 attacks got extraordinary relief from the government, in the form of legal immunity from lawsuits by the victims' families and limits on their liability coverage. As Mary Schiavo, Transportation Department inspector general from 1990 to 1996, has charged, the law was retroactively changed "to cut off the ability to engage in full discovery, and to limit victims' legal rights to punish the reckless companies that made us vulnerable to the terrorists." She points out that in the aftermath of prior terrorist attacks on airplanes, victims have been able to determine how they happened and to seek full redress from culpable parties.

"Terrorism against aviation is not an unknown, unforeseeable risk," she notes. "It is because aviation has been repeatedly attacked this way that we have laws, regulations and requirements for aviation security. . . . If your negligence leads to someone being hurt and if you do not have enough insurance, your car, house, salary and bank accounts can be seized. Why are the airlines any different—because so many have been harmed? A family's harm and suffering are not less because thousands were killed as opposed to a few dozen."

The airline industry wasn't the only example of a wealthy special interest taking advantage of the September 11 attacks to line its own pockets. Remember the anthrax crisis? Suddenly, demand for Cipro, the anthrax-fighting antibiotic made by Bayer, sky-rocketed. But it wasn't cheap. A 60-day supply of Cipro cost just under $700. However, a 60-day supply of generic ciprofloxacin cost only about $20 overseas, according to Representative Marion Berry (D-AR), the only pharmacist in Congress.

But in the fall of 2001, you couldn't buy generic Cipro in the United States. That's because Bayer held an exclusive patent on the drug that wasn't due to expire until 2003. In India, a 500-mg tablet of ciprofloxacin was selling for about five rupees, or ten cents. Here, Bayer's wholesale price was $4.67 a pill. As a bulk purchaser, the U.S. government was paying Bayer around $1.80. In Canada, the same pill cost $1.25.

Supplies of Cipro were tight that fall. In Canada, the government decided to override Bayer's Cipro patent, citing a national emergency. But the Bush Administration refused to take a similar step. Was it coincidence that two of the president's top Cabinet members are former drug company executives? Mitch Daniels, director of the Office of Management and Budget, had been a top official at Eli Lilly. Secretary of Defense Donald Rumsfeld ran G. D. Searle (now part of Pharmacia) from 1977 to 1985. He also served more recently on the board of Amylin Pharmaceuticals. In 2000 President George W. Bush was the industry's favorite politician, receiving just under a half million dollars from pharmaceuticals for his presidential campaign. Through March 29, 2004, he had reported taking in another $708,000 for his reelection bid, according to the Center for Responsive Politics.

Under intense criticism, Bayer eventually lowered the price it charged the U.S. government to 95 cents a pill. But, according to a Lehman Brothers analyst, that just reduced Bayer's profit margin on the drug from 95 percent to 65 percent. (It only costs Bayer about 20 cents to make each pill.) Bayer's giving from 1999 to present totals $840,200, 77 percent to Republicans. The company's sales of Cipro topped $1 billion in 2001 and 2002, making it one of the top 25 best-selling name-brand drugs in the country, according to drugtopics.com.

Did Congress try to step in and force Bayer to back down? No. In fact, just a few weeks after 9/11, the pharmaceutical lobby won a six-month extension on its monopoly drug patents in exchange for its agreeing to test the safety and efficacy of its products on children. Until this change, the FDA had to rely on adult studies when deciding dosages of drugs for kids, a far from ideal situation since kids metabolize drugs differently than adults. (Isn't it ridiculous that in order to enact an important public health measure Congress finds it necessary to also grant a big giveaway to industry?)

According to the Food and Drug Administration, this patent extension was worth nearly $30 billion to the industry in increased sales—about forty times the expected cost of the pediatric drug testing. All four key sponsors of the extension were top recipients of campaign cash from Big Pharma: Senator Christopher Dodd (D-CT), $377,000—number 5 lifetime among senators; Senator Mike DeWine (R-OH), $232,000—number 17; Representative Anna Eshoo (D-CA), $285,000—number 11 lifetime among House members; and Representative James Greenwood (R-PA), $180,000 —number 20. When the bill came up for a vote in the health subcommittee of the House Energy and Commerce Committee, consumer advocates failed to trim back the industry giveaway. According to Public Citizen, subcommittee members who voted to leave the patent extension untouched received 154 percent more from the drug industry in campaign contributions since 1990 than those who voted the other way. The law, known as the Best Pharmaceuticals for Children Act, was passed on a voice vote in both chambers of Congress and signed into law at the beginning of 2002.

Insured to the Hilt (on Our Dime, That Is)

The insurance industry—another huge sector of the economy—got its own specially tailored handout from the government after 9/11. Ten days after the attacks, a skulk of insurance executives met with President Bush and Commerce Secretary Donald Evans to press for the creation of a multibillion-dollar government safety net to limit their exposure to future terrorist incidents. Evans was no doubt well acquainted with two of those execs from his days as Bush campaign fundraising chairman; Maurice Greenberg of the American Insurance Group and Robert O'Connell of Massachusetts Mutual Life Insurance had each personally raised at least $100,000 for the campaign as Bush "Pioneers." Overall, according to the Center for Responsive Politics, the industry gave Bush $1.6 million for his 2000 campaign and $1.1 million for his Inaugural Committee. Since 1989 it has distributed $213.7 million overall to federal candidates and parties. (Bush raised more than $2.2 million from the insurance sector for his reelection bid as reported at the beginning of March 2004.)

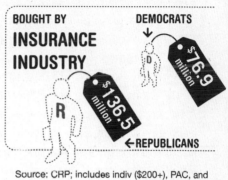

BOUGHT BY
INSURANCE
INDUSTRY

DEMOCRATS
$76.9 million

$136.5 million

R

←REPUBLICANS

Source: CRP; includes indiv ($200+), PAC, and soft-money contributions 1989–2004 to federal candidates and parties

The insurers told the White House that they faced $40 billion to $75 billion in claims from 9/11, a sum they were well equipped to handle out of their approximately $3 trillion in assets. But they claimed that they would have to stop writing insurance policies covering acts of terrorism starting in January 2002 because they couldn't adequately predict the risk of future attacks. Their sky-is-falling rhetoric convinced leaders of both parties that inaction could cripple the economy. "We're facing a cliff," Treasury Secretary Paul O'Neill testified before Congress that fall. Without the promise of future bailouts for the insurers, banks would stop lending to real-estate builders, investors would stop investing, and so on.

Some business analysts saw through the insurance industry's claims. Holman Jenkins, a *Wall Street Journal* business columnist, said, "To buy this alarum, you would have to believe real-estate lenders would wake up on Jan. 1 and decide to liquidate their businesses and end their careers. You would have to believe, against all evidence of prosperous, wartime economies, that the U.S. economy would fold up and die because financiers and entrepreneurs are too weenie to find a way to proceed despite the absence of insurance for terrorism risk." Jenkins concluded that the dire predictions of "the termination of all economic activity as we know it" is, at best, hyperbole.

Prior experience with insurance company greed should have led Congress to be more skeptical. In 1992, after Hurricane Andrew devastated Florida, Greenberg's son Jeffrey, then a VP at his father's AIG, wrote an internal memo saying that Andrew was "an opportunity to get price increases now," the *Wall Street Journal* reported. But big money has a way of inducing amnesia in almost all members of Congress.

So we the taxpayers are now the insurers of the last resort for one of the richest, most powerful and least regulated industries in America. Even though it took an extra year before the insurers got their government safety net—during which time the sky did not fall and the economy did not crash—Congress eventually passed a bill much to the industry's liking.

Department of Excess Profit Security

When the Senate voted on November 19, 2002, to create the Department of Homeland Security, Republicans prevented Senator Jon Corzine (D-NJ) from adding his chemical security proposal as an amendment, as we described in chapter 15. The EPA's tentative efforts at addressing the issue were also dead. No binding provisions regarding security at chemical plants were included in the homeland security bill, by the way. (When President Bush signed the new law, American Chemistry Council president Greg Lebedev and a top staffer were among the dignitaries invited to witness the event.)

But it wasn't as if Congress didn't have time to fine-tune the Homeland Security bill. Before passing the final version, House legislators took the straightforward bill they had passed earlier in the year and tucked a host of unrelated provisions into the version they sent to the Senate.

Thus, the revised bill included a provision limiting legal liability for companies that produce vaccines, a sop to drug manufacturer Eli Lilly, which faces lawsuits from families touting new research connecting thimerosal, a preservative used in vaccines, to autism. Another provision that sailed through the House, and ultimately the Senate, undid a ban originally sponsored by the late Senator Paul Wellstone (D-MN) on any government contracts related to homeland security going to companies that establish foreign tax havens to avoid U.S. taxes. A bipartisan who's who of ex-elected officials turned mercenaries lobbied for the amendment, including former Republican presidential candidate Bob Dole, former House Ways and Means chairman Bill Archer (R-TX), Bush family confidant Charlie Black, former House Appropriations Committee chairman Robert L. Livingston (R-LA), and former Keating Five senator Dennis DeConcini (D-AZ). Among the companies seeking the measure: Accenture, the Arthur Andersen spin-off; scandal-ridden Tyco International, and toolmaker Ingersoll-Rand.

When these and other special-interest provisions came to light, many senators complained vociferously. Democrats, along with Republican maverick John McCain (R-AZ), tried to get them excised. But they lost that fight after the White House and Republican leaders promised to tone down the offending provisions with corrective legislation in the following year. Actually, House Majority Leader Tom DeLay (R-TX) made that promise with his fingers crossed behind his back, since he stated only that he would "consider" any such changes. In the end, only the Eli Lilly provision got repealed—the Wellstone rule preventing tax evaders from getting homeland security contracts was not restored.

The Terrorism Risk Insurance Act provides up to $100 billion over three years to cover 90 percent of future terrorism-related insurance claims. Insurers would be required to repay very little or no federal assistance.

This approach was a marked departure from the original House bill, passed the prior winter, that would have required insurers to cover the first $1 billion cost of a terrorist attack, with the federal government offering long-term loans to help pay for the rest. But the insurance industry didn't want to be on the hook. It wanted direct aid and lobbied hard for a Senate version promoted by Senator Christopher Dodd (D-CT) that would have them pay for the first $10 billion of an attack out-of-pocket but then dump the rest of the cost on us taxpayers.

The Consumer Federation of America, an opponent of the measure, pointed out that the industry could afford to pay far more, having reported a 66.4 percent increase in profits in the first half of 2002. And it argued that the huge government safety net would remove the incentive for insurance companies to require better security measures from the businesses they insure, perversely making Americans less safe, not more.

But the Consumer Federation of America isn't a big donor to political campaigns. As noted above, the insurance and real estate industries are among the biggest. Senator Dodd has received $985,000 from the insurance industry during his career in the Senate, putting him at number 1 among all his colleagues in takings from that lucrative source. He called the final bill a vital "safety net" for the insurance business, a major employer in his state.

ALL THE NEWS
THAT'S FIT TO OMIT

Are you wondering where the local news went, or why a few companies are gobbling up most, if not all, of the radio stations, newspapers and even TV broadcasters in your area? It's a tale of "I'll scratch your back if you scratch mine" as some media giants cozy up to Washington politicians and get favorable treatment in return.

Twenty years ago, approximately fifty companies dominated the business of movies, music, radio, newspapers, books, magazines, TV and cable. Today, much of the control of the information and entertainment industry is concentrated in fewer then ten giant conglomerates, thanks in large degree to the wave of mergers and acquisitions unleashed by the deregulatory provisions of the 1996 Telecommunications Act, though the trend was well under way before then.

For example, the 1996 law allowed companies to own as many radio stations as they wanted, unleashing the growth of the Clear Channel conglomerate, which now owns over 1,200 stations, more than one out of ten nationwide. That's four times as many as its closest competitor, and more than forty times its original size. The result has been the wholesale elimination of local broadcast staffs in the name of efficiency, to the detriment of community service.

In Wheeling, West Virginia, where Clear Channel owns seven local stations, the company recently axed two local talk radio programs that provided much coverage of hometown issues. "They have eliminated seven-and-a-half hours of local programming," longtime WWVA news reporter Dave Demerest said. "They are leaving the public with practically no forum for discussion of local interest like the steel crisis, downtown revitalization and eminent domain in Center Wheeling. How is the public going to discuss this on the air if there are no local programs? I was told there would be considerable cuts in local news, and the amount of time devoted to local news coverage."

In Minot, North Dakota, where Clear Channel owns six of eight stations, emergency personnel couldn't reach a live person at any of the stations to warn the public during a chemical spill in 2002, the Center for Public Integrity reported. And, as the *Washington Post* noted in a long feature on the company's rise, "when the Pentagon was attacked on September 11, the [three Clear Channel] stations [in Washington] didn't have the personnel to cover the emergency in their own backyard."

As the nonprofit advocacy group Free Press points out, "The big losers of this trend are citizen access to local information—and, even more disturbing, the information needs of our democracy."

Longtime program director John Rook, a Republican who says he usually believes consolidation in business is a good idea, wrote the FCC's commissioners an open letter in which he declared, "The idea of a local voice is almost unheard of today in any of the top 200 cities." He added, "Consolidation has benefited the profits of these huge companies; however, the loss of jobs, loss of quality concerned broadcasters, loss of hundreds of businesses formerly supported by radio are not benefits."

But public-minded voices across the political spectrum don't have the clout the big media companies have in Congress. Clear Channel's PAC, its executives, and their families have given $1.2 million since 1989 to federal candidates, leadership PACs, and party committees, 75 percent to Republicans. Viacom, a giant media company that is the owner of Infinity Broadcasting, which is another radio conglomerate following in Clear Channel's footsteps, has given $5.8 million since 1989, 74 percent to Democrats. The head of Infinity Broadcasting, Mel Karmazin, said in 2001, "We were very active in lobbying for the Telecommunications Act of 1996 . . .

We were so aggressive trying to get the rules tilted our way. And by the way, we think that there's still a need for further deregulation."

Overall, the whole telecommunications sector, which includes computer and Internet-based companies, printers and publishers, telephone and telecommunications companies, and the whole entertainment world of TV, movies, and radio, has contributed $484.2 million to federal candidates and party committees since 1989.

Clear Channel also hasn't balked at directly intervening in the political process in an overtly partisan fashion. In the

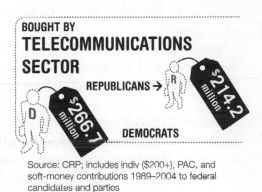

BOUGHT BY
TELECOMMUNICATIONS SECTOR

REPUBLICANS → R $214.2 million

D $266.7 million

DEMOCRATS

Source: CRP; includes indiv ($200+), PAC, and soft-money contributions 1989–2004 to federal candidates and parties

spring of 2003, Clear Channel radio stations in cities around the country organized pro-Administration demonstrations they called "Rally for America," in support of the Iraq war. The company also removed a popular singing group, the Dixie Chicks, from its playlists that spring, after one of the band's members criticized President Bush and his foreign policy. In 2001 the company pulled radio ads paid for by Democrats who wanted to criticize a Mississippi Republican congressman for failing to act in the face of rising gas prices.

In 2003 the issue of the growing concentration of media ownership exploded on the national stage, when the Federal Communications Commission voted in June to relax the rule that had prevented one TV network from owning another. It also voted to allow one network to control TV stations reaching up to 45 percent of all Americans. And it decided to loosen rules allowing a company to own a daily newspaper along with as many as three TV stations, eight radio stations and a cable system in the same market. A wide array of opponents, ranging from the AFL-CIO to the National Rifle Association criticized the proposals at public hearings, in public comments submitted to the commission, and at public protests. Advocates estimated that as many as three million people had sent a message either to Congress or the FCC to voice their concerns.

But FCC chairman Michael Powell, a Republican, scheduled only one public hearing on the rule changes. (Perhaps he wanted to save time to investigate Janet Jackson's Super Bowl "wardrobe malfunction," which he moved swiftly to address with hearings.)

Powell, a fervent advocate of deregulation, has referred to broadcast corporations as "our clients," and when asked of his concept of the "public interest," said, "I have no idea."

The public backlash against media concentration took Congress by storm last year. On July 23, a month after the FCC issued its new rules, the House voted 400–21 for restrictions on a single TV station from reaching more than 35% of Americans. Two months later, the Senate voted 55–40 to repeal all of the FCC's new regulations. Two hundred and five House members, including 11 Republicans, signed a letter to Speaker of the House Dennis Hastert (R-IL) asking him to allow that chamber to endorse the Senate's action, which he rejected. Then the big media companies went to work, engaging the White House and getting President Bush to threaten a veto if the stricter requirements on TV stations were not dropped from pending appropriations legislation. Bush has received over $473,000 in contributions from the TV, radio, and cable industries since his first run for president, more than any other federal candidate.

And thus House and Senate negotiators huddled with White House officials—with Democrats excluded from the final talks—and produced a "compromise" that canceled the reform approved by both chambers, merely setting the limit at 39 percent for how many Americans a single network could reach. "The Republicans went into a closet, met with themselves and announced a 'compromise,'" Senator Fritz Hollings (D-SC), said. "The Democrats and the conferees were ignored, and the press ought to be ashamed of calling it a 'compromise.' We weren't a part of it whatsoever."

* * * * *

"It's very simple. If you're an incumbent member of Congress and you've supported us, we're going to support you."

—Rodney Smith, lobbyist for SBC Communications, quoted in Speaking Freely, 2nd edition, CRP

The new limit, critics noted, was so high that Rupert Murdoch's News Corporation and Viacom would not have to divest any of their properties. The two companies are in the top ten of all media companies in their campaign contributions: In addition to Viacom's $5.8 million since 1989, News Corporation has given $4.3 million since 1989, 68 percent to Republicans. According to the Associated Press, they also spent a combined $5.5 million on lobbying between January 1, 2002 and June 30, 2003. Commenting on the revised rule, Gene Kimmelman, public policy director for Consumers Union, commented, "This is a sweetheart deal for Murdoch." Murdoch's Fox News is considered the most pro-administration of all the cable news channels. His flagship newspapers, the *New York Post* and the *Boston Herald,* both endorsed Bush in 2000.

As for Clear Channel, its ties to President Bush run deeper than most. The company's founder, Lowry Mays, was put on the governing board of the University of Texas Investment Management Company by Bush when he was still governor of Texas. (His term on the board expired in 2003). Bush also appointed Clear Channel vice-chairman Thomas Hicks to head the investment company's board in 1995. Under his leadership, it invested over half a billion dollars in assets run by Hicks's associates and other major Republican donors, including several with warm relationships with the Bush family dynasty like the Carlyle Group. When these insider dealings were exposed by the *Houston Chronicle* in 1999, Hicks resigned from the company's board. By then, he had made

Bush a rich man when he bought the Texas Rangers from him and his partners in 1998 for $250 million, three times their investment in the team. Bush's take was $14.9 million, almost 25 times what he originally invested. According to the Center for Public Integrity, "Hicks and [his law firm Hicks, Muse, Tate & Furst]'s employees rank nineteenth as Bush's career patrons, having given him at least $233,000."

WHAT IS TO BE DONE?

"There are two things that are important in politics. The first is money and I can't remember what the second one is."

—Senator Mark Hanna, *chair of the Republican National Committee, 1895*

Money has always played a prominent role in American politics. There's little point in debating whether things were worse a hundred years ago, when Mark Hanna—the political boss who arguably built the first modern money-raising machine by systematically tithing banks, railroads, and other major corporations in order to raise approximately $6 million to $7 million for William McKinley—made the memorable remark that opens this chapter. McKinley's money, which was the equivalent of over $145 million today, swamped the Democratic candidate William Jennings Bryan, who had one-tenth as much. As we've tried to show in this book, Big Money from a narrow and self-interested elite group of donors distorts democracy and produces perverse outcomes that favor a privileged few and hurt the rest of us in all sorts of ways.

Hasn't it always been this way? And haven't we already tried to fix it?

The short answer is yes. Politics in America has always been a contest between organized people and organized money. But that's no reason to throw up our hands and become resigned to the situation. After all, the history of America is the history of steady efforts to expand democracy and include everyone on an equal footing. The Constitution did not give women or non-property owners the right to vote. It explicitly condoned slavery by counting African-Americans as being only worth ⅗ of a vote. It made no mention of the rights of workers to vote to self-organize into unions and bargain collectively with their employers. It took no heed of the diverse needs of people with disabilities.

And yet today we take for granted that women have the right to vote, that there should be no barriers to being able to vote (like literacy tests or poll taxes), and that not only do African-Americans have the right to vote, the federal government has a special responsibility to insure that past discriminatory practices are not continued. The march toward a fully representative and participatory democracy is obviously not complete, and today there are vital questions being raised about re-enfranchising former felons who have paid their debt to society, expanding representation by experimenting with proportional systems (such as instant-runoff voting and fusion), replacing the Electoral College with a direct popular vote, and so on. But change that opens up the political system to greater and more equitable participation is not only possible, it is the American story.

Toward a Solution: Clean Money, Clean Elections

To date, major campaign reforms have centered on refining the system of disclosure and limits. However, in Maine, Arizona, North Carolina, New Mexico and Vermont, citizens are trying a bold new model for electing their representatives. Instead of fine-tuning the system by which candidates collect private money, candidates are given another option for running a viable campaign, one that does not make them beholden to special interest contributors.

Under Clean Money campaign reform, also known as Clean Elections, candidates who voluntarily agree to limit their spending and to reject campaign contributions from private sources can qualify for grants of full public financing for their campaigns. Primaries are covered as well as general elections, opening up the possibility for real competition within the parties, which is a critical element in reducing the dominance of money in elections. Additional funds are also made available, up to a limit, if a Clean Money candidate is outspent by a privately financed opponent.

In Arizona, nine out of eleven statewide elected officials, including the governor, secretary of state, attorney general, treasurer, and mine inspector, and four out of five members of the corporations commission, got elected running "clean" in either 2000 or 2002. Aside from a very modest infusion of seed money at the start of their campaigns, the largest campaign contribution these public representatives had to collect was a $5 check. Once they qualified, by collecting a fairly large number of these $5 contributions, they agreed to abide by spending limits and appear in debates, in return receiving public funds—up to $2.3 million in the case of the winning gubernatorial candidate, Janet Napolitano.

In Maine, 77 percent of the state senate and 55 percent of the state house is made up of Democrats and Republicans who ran "clean," along with one Green and three independents. The Arizona state house is 45 percent "clean," as is 17 percent of the state senate. Overall, 152 out of 287 state elected officials in the two states, or 53 percent, participated in Clean Elections in 2002.

In case after case, candidates of all political stripes who run "clean" say that being freed of the money chase has helped them pay more attention to ordinary constituents and their needs. "It's a good way of giving government back to the people. . . . It lets people who are not well-connected run for the legislature," says Republican Senator Ed Youngblood, of Maine, who defeated a longtime, powerful incumbent when he ran for office.

"The first thing people asked me about was my running 'clean.' 'Oh my goodness, a politician who is in no one's pocket!' They couldn't believe it," says Representative Sue Hawes (D-ME).

The day in the spring of 2002 that then–Arizona attorney general Janet Napolitano dropped off her qualifying contributions and nominating petitions, she said, "I feel like I just completed a final exam. It's been a great grass-roots Phase I of the campaign. You don't have to come to a $250-a-plate dinner to take part. Most people can afford $5 and can invest in a candidate for governor." She told the *Arizona Republic*, "I sat in my office for five or six hours a day asking people for money when I ran for attorney general [in 1998]. This is definitely the wave of the future."

That November, Napolitano became the first governor anywhere in America elected without relying on large contributions from private special interest donors. And one of her first steps was to sign an executive order creating a discount prescription drug program for seniors. She has told supporters that if she hadn't run "clean," then she surely would have come under pressure from contributors representing pharmaceutical interests urging her to either shelve the program or modify it to suit their interests. But none of that happened, and today thousands of seniors who are Medicare beneficiaries are receiving lower-cost prescription drugs as a result.

Clean Election incumbents in Maine and Arizona's legislatures report a greater feeling of independence from special interests and more freedom to speak their minds. "The business lobbyists left me alone," said state Representative Glenn Cummings (D-ME), who was the first candidate in the country to qualify for Clean Elections funding back in 2000. "I think they assumed I was unapproachable. It sure made it easier to get through the hallways on the way to a vote!" Beth Edmonds, another Democratic state senator from Maine, agrees that the new system has changed life in the statehouse. Edmonds, the chair of the senate's labor committee, recalls the debate over a bill to give more overtime to truckers. "All the trucking companies were in my committee room. The truckers themselves weren't there. But I know I haven't taken a penny from the companies and they know that too. None of them have any ownership of me."

Representative Meg Burton Cahill (D-AZ), laughed as she thought about one episode from her first term after running "clean." "A lobbyist here, the most powerful in the state, said I treated him badly because I met with him on an issue and simply said I would take his information into consideration along with the opposing view that I had already heard. He wasn't used to that!" Of course, an incumbent who is not carrying a big campaign debt or worrying about how they will finance their next race is in a very different position than the typical elected official most lobbyists are used to dealing with.

Republican Marc Spitzer, a member of the Arizona Corporation Commission who got elected while participating in Clean Elections, summed up the law's benefits, saying, "I am not a novice campaigner, having run for office successfully four times under traditional private financing and in 2000 under Arizona's Clean Elections law. The comparison is stark.

Clean Elections empowers the constituency, gives voices to thousands of voters, expands opportunities and enhances democracy. Clean Elections is about bringing back grass-roots, one-to-one politics, the way it used to be, instead of high-dollar media campaigns financed by huge contributions from the well-heeled. Clean Elections is about the restoration of democracy."

Versions of Clean Money have also passed in New Mexico, North Carolina, and Vermont, and more states are considering it. Reformers in Connecticut, Hawaii, Illinois, Maryland, Minnesota, and Wisconsin are well on their way to winning similar systems. The states have always been laboratories of democracy, and as more of them adopt systems of comprehensive public financing, the day grows closer that this change will become a reality for elections to Congress and the White House as well. "Clean Money, Clean Elections" legislation modeled on these state systems has been introduced in the House of Representatives by Representative John Tierney (D-MA), building on an earlier bill written by Senators Paul Wellstone (D-MN) and John Kerry (D-MA).

Real change is possible. Money in politics doesn't always have to hurt average people. If the money comes from us, the people, that is. After all, he who pays the piper calls the tune. If someone is going to own the politicians, it might as well be us.

HOW TO GET INVOLVED

1. **Join with national and state activists working for real change. Visit Public Campaign's Web site at www.publicampaign.org for more information.**

2. **Sign up to receive "OUCH! How Money in Politics Hurts You," our free e-mail bulletin, by going to www.publicampaign.org/ouch**

3. **Learn more about money in politics. Resources we recommend:**

   - **The Center for Responsive Politics: www.opensecrets.org**

   - **The National Institute for Money in State Politics: www.followthemoney.org**

   - **The Center for Public Integrity: www.public-i.org**

   - **The Color of Money Project: www.colorofmoney.org**

4. **Sign the Lincoln Call for a Presidency Of, By and For the People by going to www.publicampaign.org/lincolncall, and ask others to sign up, too.**

INDEX

Page numbers in *italics* indicate graphic displays or sidebar quotes.

JOIN THE LINCOLN CALL
FOR A PRESIDENCY OF, BY, AND FOR THE PEOPLE!

One hundred forty years after Lincoln's address at Gettysburg, the principles of American democracy are endangered by a cascade of special interest money. A government of, by, and for the people, as President Abraham Lincoln said seven score years ago, is threatened by a money-driven political system that makes donors and their dollars count for more than voters and their votes.

Nowhere are the dangers to these principles more apparent than in the race for the White House. The presidency is the only office that is supposed to belong equally to each and every one of us. Yet our would-be leaders are required by this process to spend too much time raising money from a small group of contributors who too often want something in return.

What is needed is a system of full public financing that puts voters first. Models for such a law are already working well in Maine and Arizona.

Our leaders should be chosen by the people in voting booths, and no one else. Americans are fed up with the high cost of campaigning and the high price we pay when special interest money dominates public policy debates. Join with other patriots by adding your name to a call for an end of government of, by, and for the wealthy special interests.

Sign up on the web by going to: **www.publicampaign.org/lincolncall**
– or –
For more information, write to us at:
Public Campaign
1320 19th St., NW
Suite M-1
Washington, DC 20036